PENGUIN BOOKS

LIVING TO TELL THE TALE

Jane Taylor McDonnell teaches at Carleton College, where she directed the Women's Studies program for many years and where she now teaches a writing and reading class called "Witness Narratives; Memoirs of Survival." She is the author of *News from the Border*, a "mother's memoir" about her autistic son. The book has been translated into Italian, German, and Portuguese and won the Minnesota Book Award for Nonfiction in 1994. She continues to speak widely on the subject of autism, and she is working on a second memoir about the last illness and death of her father.

≈ ≈ ≈

LIVING TO
TELL THE TALE

~~~

A Guide to Writing Memoir

Jane Taylor McDonnell

FOREWORD BY VIVIAN GORNICK

PENGUIN BOOKS

PENGUIN BOOKS
Published by the Penguin Group
Penguin Putnam Inc., 375 Hudson Street,
New York, New York 10014, U.S.A.
Penguin Books Ltd, 27 Wrights Lane,
London W8 5TZ, England
Penguin Books Australia Ltd, Ringwood,
Victoria, Australia
Penguin Books Canada Ltd, 10 Alcorn Avenue,
Toronto, Ontario, Canada M4V 3B2
Penguin Books (N.Z.) Ltd, 182–190 Wairau Road,
Auckland 10, New Zealand

Penguin Books Ltd, Registered Offices:
Harmondsworth, Middlesex, England

First published in Penguin Books 1998

10 9 8 7 6 5 4 3

Copyright © Jane Taylor McDonnell, 1998
Foreword copyright © Vivian Gornick, 1998
All rights reserved

Grateful acknowledgment is made for permission to reprint excerpts
from the following copyrighted works:
"Note from the Dead" by Sebastian Barry. Originally appeared in
Invisible Dublin, edited by Dermot Bolger (Raven Arts Press, 1991).
By permission of the author.
Object Lessons: The Life of the Woman and the Poet in Our Time by
Eavan Boland. Copyright © 1995 by Eavan Boland. Reprinted by
permission of W. W. Norton & Company, Inc.
Angela's Ashes: A Memoir by Frank McCourt. Copyright © 1996 by
Frank McCourt. Reprinted with the permission of Scribner,
a division of Simon & Schuster.
News from the Border by Jane Taylor McDonnell
(Ticknor & Fields, 1993). By permission of the author.
This Boy's Life by Tobias Wolff. Copyright © 1989 by Tobias Wolff.
Used by permission of Grove/Atlantic, Inc.

LIBRARY OF CONGRESS CATALOGING IN PUBLICATION DATA
McDonnell, Jane Taylor.
    Living to tell the tale: a guide to writing memoir/Jane Taylor
    McDonnell; foreword by Vivian Gornick.
        p.   cm.
    Includes bibliographical references (p.   ).
    ISBN 0 14 02.6530 9
    1. Autobiography—Authorship.   2. Biography as a literary form.
3. Report writing.   I. Title.
CT25.M34   1998
808'.06692—dc21   97–34341

Printed in the United States of America
Set in New Baskerville
Designed by Helene Berinsky

Except in the United States of America, this book is sold subject to
the condition that it shall not, by way of trade or otherwise, be lent,
re-sold, hired out, or otherwise circulated without the publisher's prior
consent in any form of binding or cover other than that in which it is
published and without a similar condition including this condition
being imposed on the subsequent purchaser.

For my family
Jim, Paul, and Kate

Foreword

BEGINNING WITH AUGUSTINE, memoir writing has given trouble, and to this day readers and writers alike seem preoccupied with trying to puzzle out the genre: Does it tell the truth or just give the facts? Report a life or set the record straight? Do journalism or make art? Inevitably, if the memoir is so good that it "reads like a novel," one hears the confused assertion that every act of writing is an act of invention so, really, autobiography is just another way of making fiction. Not so. A memoir is a work of nonfiction.

But it is true that the concerns of the memoirist are the same as those of the novelist. Memoir writing shares with fiction writing the obligation to lift from the raw material of life a tale that will shape experience, transform an event, deliver wisdom. It differs from fiction writing in the way it approaches the task, the chief difference being that a fictional "I" can be, and often is, an unreliable narrator; the nonfictional "I" can never be. In memoir, the reader must be persuaded that the narrator is speaking truth.

Truth in a memoir is achieved not through a recital of actual events; it is achieved when the reader comes to believe that the writer is working hard to engage with the experience at hand. What happened to the memoirist is not what matters; it matters only what the memoirist *makes* of what happened. For that, the power of a writing imagination is required. As V. S. Pritchett once said of the genre, "It's all in the art. You get no credit for living." The situation may be revealing, but it's the writing that provides revelation; and revelation comes only with a story well told.

In every work of literature there's a situation and a story. The situation is the context or circumstance, sometimes the plot; the story is the emotional insight that preoccupies the writer. In his *Confessions*, Augustine tells the tale of his conversion to Christianity; that's the situation. In this tale, he moves from an inchoate to a coherent sense of being, from an idling existence into a purposeful one, from a state of ignorance to one of truth; that's the story.

Inevitably, it is a story of self-discovery and self-definition. The subject of autobiography is always self-definition. That is, definition out in the world, not in the void. The memoirist, like the poet and the novelist, must engage with the world because engagement makes experience, experience makes wisdom, and finally it's the wisdom that counts. Every writer has to persuade the reader that he or she knows something and is writing as honestly as possible to arrive at what that something is.

The questions are always the same: What is the situation, and what is the story? What is the experience being shaped, the insight expressed, the self revealed? These questions are asked of the nonfictional witness as well as of the fictional storyteller.

Jane McDonnell—herself a student, practitioner, and teacher of memoir writing—has a strong grasp of the issues that dominate today's discussion of an honorable and little understood genre. The book she has written is a fine and useful introduction to the complexity of the form: its pleasures, its perils, its immense possibilities. Step by lucid step, *Living to Tell the Tale* opens the reader to the excitement and alarm of translating into shaped experience a story taken from one's very own life.

One of the most appealing elements of this book is derived from McDonnell's acute understanding that teaching people how to think like writers about events and circumstances in which they were principal actors turns out to be as dramatic an exercise as the attempt at psychoanalysis: fraught with anxiety, a struggle to focus, difficult to achieve distance, and painfully hard to identify the *real* story.

The would-be memoirist can do no better than to have Jane McDonnell for a guide. The chapter headings alone tell us how well she understands the project—"Talking Back to Your Inner Censor"; "Learning to Remember"; "How to Find Your Plot"; "To Tell or Not to Tell"—and what sort of an inner journey she is asking her student memoirists to go on. She knows that "what happened" is the least of it. She wants her readers to go down into themselves as far as they can, and stay there as long as possible.

Living to Tell the Tale is the work of a gifted teacher: her knowledge is deep, her style patient, her inclination compassionate. She's been where you are now, she knows how to help you go forward.

Vivian Gornick

Acknowledgments

I AM VERY GRATEFUL to all the students who have taken my class, "Witness Narratives; Memoirs of Survival," over the years that I have taught it at Carleton College. They have helped me think through the issues of personal writing, particularly writing about difficult events. I am especially indebted to the following who gave me permission to quote from their works: Rachel Bercovitz, Jessica Dockter, Sarah Kaplowitz, and Dominic Saucedo. Special thanks go to my friends, Sigrund Leonhard and Damgar Tisdale, and to my daughter, Kate McDonnell, for allowing me to quote from their writings. I am also very grateful to the Prose Writers group at Carleton for advice and support.

I want to acknowledge the gracious and thoughtful help given by my editor at Penguin, Caroline White, and the enthusiasm, creativity and plain hard work of my agent, Gloria Norris, without whom this book would not have been written. Thanks as well to Jane Von Mehren of Viking Penguin who helped with this book. I am also very grateful to Vivian Gornick for writing the Foreword and for leading the way in her wonderful writing class at the Loft in Minneapolis many years ago.

Contents

~ *Contents*

Introduction

NECESSARY FICTIONS OF THE SELF

WRITING IS A SECOND CHANCE at life. Although we can never go back in time to change the past, we can re-experience, interpret, and make peace with our past lives. When we write a personal narrative we find new meanings and, at the same time, we discover connections with our former selves. I think all writing constitutes an effort to establish our own meaningfulness, even in the midst of sadness and disappointment. In fact, writing sometimes seems to me to be the only way to give shape to life, to complete the process which is merely begun by living.

This book is intended to help you start to write a memoir, or perhaps to finish a piece of writing already begun. It is about learning to trust your inner narrative voice, getting through the hard times in writing, and learning to "listen" to the story itself. I hope that you will find enough ideas, examples of effective writing, exercises, and just plain inspiration to help any writer who has "lived to tell the tale."

THE OTHER DAY I watched some children play near my house:

"Bang, bang. You're dead."

"No, I'm not."

"Yes you are. I shot you."

"No, I'm not dead. I decide whether I'm dead or not."

This second child was asserting something fundamental. He wanted to tell the story in his own way, and he was saying he was the writer of his own life, of his own script. In some sense, we are all (those of us lucky enough to survive) writers of our own lives, whether it is externally in play, as these children demonstrated, or internally as we move through our day.

We have in our heads that inner voice which narrates the story of our lives. Sometimes you may be most aware of it as you fall asleep at night, or perhaps in a moment of crisis you discover that you are "talking" yourself through a difficult time. It isn't enough just to live a life; we must be continually explaining it to ourselves, sorting, remembering, casting out the less important stuff, interpreting, sometimes justifying ourselves to ourselves.

Through memoir we can effectively capture this

inner voice. Sometimes I think of memoir as the extended-prose-narrative equivalent of the lyric voice which we find in poetry. The same poetic intensity, immediacy, reliance on vivid imagery, and direct appeal to the reader are often found in the modern memoir. Sometimes the voice sounds more like a historian, or a letter writer, or maybe even like the voice-over commentator of a documentary film. Whatever your own inner voice sounds like, you can learn to capture it and transcribe it onto the page. And when you do, you will feel a satisfaction unlike anything you have ever felt before; your life will add up to more than the living of it ever did.

I haven't always lived by that belief. For a long time I kept a postcard message on my office door at the college where I have taught for the past twenty-six years. It read something like this: THE GREATEST POVERTY IS NOT BEING ABLE TO WRITE, AND HAVING OTHERS WRITE YOUR STORY FOR YOU. I'm not quite sure why I kept it up on my office door for so long. It's true I had taught English literature for some years, and later, when I began to teach Women's Studies, I wanted my students to see the saying on my door as they came to my office for conferences. They sometimes struggled over their own writing, and I wanted them to know I was thinking of them—as well as of the literature of minority American writers we were discovering together at the time.

But something else drew me to this little motto. I

3

was uneasily aware that I myself was not writing; I was not living up to the standards I had set for my students. As I encouraged them to write, as I talked of the human need to tell our stories, I was denying something very important in myself. I knew this, but couldn't quite bring it to full consciousness for many years.

I grew up in a writing family. Or maybe it would be more accurate to say it was a family of bad writers and failed (good) writers. My father, grandfather, one aunt, a great-uncle, myself—we all wrote as children and we all passed through times of intimidation as adults. That is, all except the great-uncle who made a career of writing rather bad historical novels. Uncle Rob lived for years in New York and was, I later learned, an intimate of J. Edgar Hoover. His favorite subject was Mary, Queen of Scots and his greatest triumph was seeing his book turned into an Italian opera.

I remember visiting him as a child, being marched dutifully across the southern town where my father's family lived. His house—no more than a peeling shack leaning against a filling station—was full of antiques, a huge Chippendale highboy, Hepplewhite chairs, cathedral glass, a stereopticon (with pictures of the Leaning Tower of Pisa), and the most wonderful little trinkets I had ever seen. I was usually given a small token, perhaps an engraved gold hatchet that once hung from a great-grandfather's watch fob. Sometimes I lost the little trinket when we were outside the door. On one frightening occasion, my nervousness as a child and my eagerness to please all the adults around me somehow caused me to drop the hatchet into a deep sidewalk crack just outside his door. There was an anxious moment as we all tried to fish it out, without being seen from the window.

Uncle Rob was the writer. The rest of us just wanted to be writers, never quite daring to live the kind of life which my great-uncle managed to turn into a legend even during his own lifetime. He finally retired to his little southern town, now a large city, and spent his "declining" years writing venomous letters to the editor of the local newspaper. He also began writing poetry. There was one particularly sentimental poem, about a family plantation home, which was almost saved by a wonderful image of peacocks freezing their toes on a cold winter's night.

Uncle Rob lived to be one hundred and four, and deeded all his treasures to the plantation house. On his deathbed in a nursing home, he was never told that all the antiques (except the Chippendale highboy which was simply too heavy) had been cleared out of the house, next to the Texaco station, and loaded onto a truck by robbers in the dead of one hot southern night.

My grandfather wrote stories and family records to be passed on to his children and grandchildren. My father took up writing little books when he was a child. A famous one that luckily was saved began with the memorable lines: "The sun rose in all its gorgeous and glory. I asked my parents if I could go to Africa. They said 'Yes, but be careful.' " All during my childhood, we quoted those lines. Whenever my brother and I asked to do something a little risky, the reply was often the wry "Yes, but be careful." Thus the stories we each wrote became a part of family lore; the written was woven into the lived experience.

Every summer when I was growing up, I started writing a new novel. Usually I never got past the first chapter or two. The illustrations, full-page and placed every other page, slowed me down. For my reading, I favored Victorian children's books, especially the ones in which children died. The demise of Beth in *Little Women* was, of course, read over and over, but I preferred *The Byrd's Christmas Carol*, because that book dared to kill off the heroine herself.

Needless to say, these books didn't provide very good models for my own writing. Furthermore, persistent feelings of inadequacy—briefly banished during high school and college, where I took every writing class available and edited the literary journal—kept me from writing. Later I needed to make a living, and then I had children and still needed to make a living. Perhaps I simply couldn't imagine a writer's life as my own. Maybe the image of Uncle Rob showing me the "Maestro's" letter, about the Italian opera of Mary, Queen of Scots was too foreign an image for me to apply to myself.

Eventually, later in life than many people, in my

forties in fact, I did start to write. And as I look back
on this time, it is obvious to me that I was impelled
by a crisis to start to put things down on paper. I
found myself the mother of an autistic son, more ver-
bal and capable than most, but also a child who suffered in a way I had never witnessed before. Life itself
and everything about it—learning to speak, trying to figure people out, coping with other children
who sometimes teased him relentlessly, dealing with
change—were sometimes impossibly difficult for
Paul. And the rest of us—myself, my husband and
daughter, as well as our extended families—all suffered with him.

I think that what we all experienced was a kind of
fracturing of the self. At times my whole life seemed
permeated with conflict and ambiguity. One summer
Paul was fifteen and suicidal. We placed him in an Ado-
lescent Day Treatment program where he started intensive therapy and treatment with antidepressants, but
even so, we all felt we were teetering on an edge. I took
out one of my many empty notebooks, pasted a hopeful
picture of pink peonies on the cover (my grandmother
had been famous for her peonies and they meant safety
and luck to me) and I started to write.

I wrote first thing in the morning on the back
porch, as the early sun picked out each fine spider's
thread across the wet grass. I wrote over a bitter cup of
coffee in the hospital cafeteria where Paul was a patient and in the hot car in the parking lot as I waited to

drive him home. Knowing that I could indeed lose him, I wrote first to hold on to my son, and then to hold on to to the last fifteen years of my own life.

It wasn't long, however, before I discovered that I wrote to let go as well as to hold on. I knew I must face the real possibility that I could lose Paul and I wanted to prepare myself for the unimaginable. But I also wanted the last fifteen years spent raising children to add up to something even if I lost him. I wanted to establish my own meaningfulness in the midst of sorrow. And I wanted to refuse the temptations of despair. Finally I began to know for myself what I had been telling my students for so many years.

I learned still more from writing another narrative several years later. This time I wrote about my father's last illness and death from brain cancer. When I began to write about my father's loss, at the age of almost ninety-five, of everything that had kept him so vividly alive for so many years, I was plunged once again into the same almost unbearable situation as witness. My father's brain cancer took away his eyesight and his written language; then, it took away his spoken language, his love of music, and finally his sense of time and of space.

Thus twice I felt I was "chosen" to tell a painful story. Furthermore, in both cases I had to be, at least partly, just a watcher, a bystander, a witness to a pain I could neither comprehend nor assuage. Both times when I started to write, I began to realize that the

very things which helped me to write these books—
my capacity for language, for imagined truth, and my
memory—were not available in the same way to my
son or to my father. It therefore seemed all the more
important that I tell these stories.

Always during this time I was reading memoirs. For
years before this, I had looked down on memoirs or
autobiographies as somehow inferior to fiction. Because these books proported to tell the "truth" I
thought of them as relatively naive, as simple transcrip-
tions of life. "Real" literature was fiction or poetry.

Now suddenly, I found myself seeking out
memoirs—especially those that were personal testi-
monies to survival. I searched the shelves of bookstores for personal accounts of grief and loss, of
mental illness, of addiction and recovery, accounts of
AIDS, mothers' accounts of handicapped children,
books written by deaf people and by the children of
deaf parents, books by doctors and neurologists. I
searched for autobiographical books about childhood, finding Tobias Wolff's *This Boy's Life*, Vivian Gornick's *Fierce Attachments*, Patricia Hampl's *A Romantic
Education*, Annie Dillard's *An American Childhood*.

Many of these books seemed to me to be as good
(in a literary sense) as any of the novels I was reading
at the time. Some of them, of course, were by well-
known writers who had also written novels or poems,
but now felt the need to tell some part of their story
in a different form. But others were written by people

who were simply driven by the need to bear witness to their survival. In almost all of them I discovered something of value to myself personally, as well as to myself as writer and as teacher. But because of the "racking" or shelving conventions of the book trade, I found many of these memoirs scattered around bookstores: under parenting, health, travel, or family, for example.

Soon I started to teach a college course called "Witness Narratives; Memoirs of Survival" in which I introduced my students to some of the most moving of these books: Natalie Kusz's *Road Song*, Eva Hoffman's *Lost in Translation*, Maya Angelou's *I Know Why the Caged Bird Sings*, Lucy Grealy's *Autobiography of a Face*. I taught short pieces by Tim O'Brien, James Baldwin, and Mary McCarthy. I recommended dozens of other books and made a place in the class for students to write their own personal narratives.

Among my undergraduate students over the years there have been many who have written about their experiences with childhood sexual abuse, about their struggles with anorexia, about their parents' divorce, about the suicide of a classmate. Over and over again I have been amazed that they could write about such experiences when still so young. They seemed to have found not only the courage to confront such experiences in writing, but also the wisdom to begin to see the shape of such a story, how to tell it to others who have not experienced it directly.

ONE OF THE THINGS I learned in teaching my class (and in writing my own personal narratives) was that, even with all the attention it has received lately, the "crisis memoir" (as most contemporary memoirs seem to be) has rarely been explored in depth, or even sufficiently valued as the rich and complex form that it is. This is true, even though we are experiencing a kind of literary renascence in personal writing at this moment in time. The personal essay, journals and diaries, autobiographical writing, and especially what is now called "fictive autobiography," as well as the memoir and creative nonfiction in all its forms, are making a comeback.

From Maxine Hong Kingston's *The Woman Warrior* to Frank McCourt's *Angela's Ashes*, the memoir of an individual's survival has become a contemporary form that is enjoying immense new popularity. So prominent is the literary memoir that it has been the featured subject of *The New York Times Magazine* and *The Women's Review of Books*. Again and again, we are reminded that the writer who might earlier have written an autobiographical novel is now writing frankly in the first person, engaging the reader directly and intimately with an account of his or her own life history.

Furthermore, in the last ten years there have been published hundreds of books which might be called crisis narratives or memoirs of survival—stories of illness, abuse, emigration, cultural dislocations of all sorts. In fact, one writer on personal narrative claims that "every autobiography is a story of crisis, in that it recounts change, turning points, conversions, critical lettings-go and breaks with the past . . ." (Chandler, page 9)

All writing is in some way therapeutic. And although the main intention of this book is not to provide help in getting through crises, I do recognize that some of the insights learned in a therapeutic setting also apply to the processes of writing (and vice versa). The crisis narrative obviously has its beginnings in the therapeutic impulse, in the desire to bear witness to some painful truth experienced either individually or collectively, in the wish to tell in order, finally, to heal. Likewise, the insights gained through writing will always help us in living our lives.

Traumatic events, however, call into question the very issues which personal writing explores: the construction of the self, attachment to others, assumptions of safety, and, perhaps most importantly of all, a sense of the meaningful order of creation, as Judith Herman notes, in her book *Trauma and Recovery*. In this kind of writing the narrative act is an act of recovery in both senses of the word: recovery of memories which have been lost or partly lost, and reconstitution of a lost or broken self. This self, having been in some way fragmented or dislocated, both recovers and *is* recovered.

Philip Roth, who wrote a memoir about his father's last illness and death, has written: "We are all writing fictitious versions of our lives all the time, contradictory but mutually entangling stories that, however subtly or grossly falsified, constitute our hold on reality and are the closest thing we have to truth."

Many things, however, can happen to disrupt our inner flow of narrative, our necessary fictions of the self. The inner narrative we experience from the time we first know ourselves to be selves, the voice in our heads which speaks to us more or less continually— sorting, arranging, interpreting, and making sense of our lives—is a very fragile voice. Grief and loss, addictions, major illness, imprisonment, war—these and many other experiences can cause us not only to forget memories, but also to lose our trust in other people, as well as our trust in a dependable "reality" or the "meaningfulness of creation." As such crises force us to question inherited and communal values, we may lose for a while our very ways of explaining ourselves to ourselves. Many of the narratives discussed here (both published and unpublished) grow out of experiences of crisis. They may deal with large subjects, but they deal with them in immediate and comprehensible ways.

Furthermore, many narratives of crisis actually explore a fractured self. As they speak of the experience, they also reflect on how the experience is perceived and remembered (or misremembered) by the teller. Often, especially when illness or cultural dislocation is involved, they question basic assumptions about language and the nature of reality. Sometimes they even consider how the story can (and cannot) be told.

In fact, one of the major attractions of contemporary memoirs is that they not only "show" and "tell," give scenes and summary, but they also reflect on the very process of telling itself. These books show an "examined life" in a particular sense of the word. A flexible form of writing, memoir can combine the techniques of fiction with essay writing, the personal with the public dimensions of an experience, and the documentary account with poetic and evocative recreations of experience. A dramatic story can be told, but there is also room for reflection on memory and the imagination and on the creation of a sense of self in the world.

Of course in all of this, the very act of writing is a part of recovery. In the telling, the writer becomes a survivor—one who has changed, but lived to tell the tale. These narratives, and the one you may wish to write, seek to reconstitute the lost self and reconceive the traumatizing experience as a survivor's story. In them the more mature writer can reflect with profound sympathy on that earlier self which suffered but did not yet know the meaning of the suffering. Furthermore, the best examples of this kind of writing are more than just private. They are also deeply spiritual and historical accounts that bear witness to some universal trauma experienced on a personal level.

14

———

So WHY have I written this book? you might ask. For one thing, it is the kind of book I (and others I know) have been searching for in bookstores. As I was writing my own personal narratives, I found many relevant classes and workshops, but no books which sufficiently valued this kind of writing or offered advice on handling the problems specific to first-person narrative. No guidebook that I could find explored the intimate connections between memory and imagination, or the ethical issues of writing about other people's roles in our own lives, or the fictional strategies which can be used in shaping memoir. As far as I know, there have been no guides for the writer who wishes to turn a story of survival into a work of creative nonfiction. I hope, therefore, that this book will both introduce you to the richness of this literary form and offer inspiration for your own writing.

I will attempt to help you in several different ways. One is to identify common problems and doubts encountered in writing personal narrative, such as the seeming inadequacy of memory, questions about the place of the imagination in a truthful account, or concerns about how to plot an "already known" series of events. I will draw on my own experience as a writer of memoir, partly because that is what I know best, but also because I believe we each encounter similar problems.

And to show how others have dealt with difficulties

15

in writing, I will give examples from both published writers and student pieces. In each case I will try to make explicit the strategies they used to overcome various problems in writing personal narratives. Every chapter will end with practical exercises intended to help you over the trouble spots. The first half of the book should help you to generate material (and to turn off the inner censors to allow you to get on with the job). The second half of the book will introduce you to many techiques which you can use as you shape your story. A suggested reading list at the end of the book recommends recent memoirs on many different subjects.

By the end of the book you will, I hope, begin to learn to trust the memories you have retained, to find other "documentary" sources such as letters or family photos or medical records to supplement sketchy memories, to use your imagination to speculate about a past you cannot remember or know, and finally to apply some techniques of fiction writing to your non-fiction writing.

I call all of this learning to "listen to the story." Such respectful "listening" ultimately has to do with letting go and allowing the true subject to emerge. It happens only later, after we have done a lot of hard work. But there does come a time—and I hope this book will testify to the possibility of that time—when suddenly the scales fall from our eyes and we begin to see. There is a story there! It has a shape and a subject. It is your story and it speaks to others.

BACK TALK

Getting Started by Talking Back to Your Inner Censors

IN THE INTRODUCTION I talked about the inner voice we have in our heads which narrates the course of our lives for us. I implied that we need to start listening to that voice if we want to write. I didn't mention, however, another kind of speaker which intrudes all too often: that of our inner censor, the editorializing voice which points out what is wrong, not what is right about us. All writers must, at some point, confront these negative messages, but memoir writers may face particularly strong prohibitions. After all, the form demands both honesty and creativity, scrupulous attention to outer reality, as well as faithfulness to an inner vision. We are impelled to write because we have some personal story we want to share with others, yet we are often afraid of telling it the wrong way or of offending others who have been a part of our own story.

In *Bird By Bird,* Anne Lamott identifies a couple of real stinkers in her own head: "First there's the vinegar-lipped Reader Lady, who says primly 'Well, *that's* not very interesting, is it?' And there's the emaciated German male who writes these Orwellian memos detailing your thought crimes. And there are your parents. . . ." (Page 26) Now think for a moment about the voices in your own head which tell you you can't write and shouldn't even dream of trying to set anything down on paper. Maybe it is your ex-husband who was in the habit of telling you you couldn't write (possibly because he came home and found a cold stove). Or it was your mother who thought you should be out mowing the lawn before guests came for dinner, not sitting out on the roof of the chicken house writing gloomy poems.

You may wonder why I am telling you first off that you need to listen to the "vinegar-lipped Reader Lady" or her cronies. After all, don't we want to shut up these voices? You will see, however, that we need to give those voices a place. And then we need to firmly shut them away out of sight.

Naming the Inner Censors

Whenever I start to teach a class of students who want to write personal narratives, I ask them to name their inner censors. I invite them to voice their fears, which they soon discover are really everybody's fears. One of the first things they always mention is the assumption that their own experience isn't significant enough. Some even go so far as to say that nothing "big" has ever happened to them. One student told the class that nothing very important had ever happened to her; then during the break I overheard her telling another student about being held hostage in her high school library by another student who had become psychotic.

I joined the conversation and pointed out that this event *was* significant and could become a vivid written piece. As she told it, the story was very funny; she hadn't been really frightened, the other student wasn't armed and he just wanted to ramble on about the FBI or the CIA. She felt sad for him, but she also minimized the importance of the event for herself. In the end, she wrote a wonderful narrative about another high school friend who died, not about the hostage-taking student.

Perhaps my student didn't want to tell the story of the hostage-taking because it really was not as important to her as the story of the friend who died. Or it may be that she couldn't see the shape of the hostage story, and therefore couldn't imagine it written. In any case, she got beyond the feeling that nothing significant had ever happened to her.

There are other common worries. Almost every-

one feels a special pressure to be honest and trustworthy, and just as importantly, to be *perceived* as
honest and trustworthy. We all want both to be believed and to sound believable. For this reason, my
students and I often discuss the reliability of the voice
of the narrator in various published pieces we read
together. They are very quick to notice any falseness
of tone, and are especially wary of any suggestion of
sentimentality. In identifying these problems in other
writers, they voice common concerns about how their
own writing might be perceived by others.

As you read the work of others, you might ask
yourself: does the writer seem too detached, inappro-
priately ironical, or evasive? Does he or she skip over
or minimize something important? Your own re-
sponses to other people's writing will become very important as you work through your own writing.

My students name other fears as well. Some will
admit that writing a personal narrative about some
traumatic event can heighten the temptation to write
a revenge narrative. In fact, many people are afraid
they might appear to be writing only as an act of self-
justification. Insisting on too much "specialness," act-
ing the part of the tragedy king or queen, perversely
feeding on one's grief or anger or depression and
refusing to get over it—all of these are pitfalls of
memoir writing and are often feared by the beginning
writer. Such fears may be behind the concern that
one's own experience isn't "significant" enough, that

20

we might simply be insisting on our own specialness out of egotistical self-preoccupation—and that our readers might dismiss us for that very reason.

My students often say they don't remember enough, or they fear that their memories may be false or incomplete or inaccurate. And so on. I'm sure you can name a dozen other reasons why you can't write—or shouldn't write. So what should you do now?

First of all, I suggest that you actively confront those inner censors. Stop and listen to the voice and write it down. Here is what a student of mine wrote:

Memoir writing is all about waiting until the scary seems safe enough to write about.

But the problem is that you want the reader to feel the scariness come out of the words on the page.

You want to make the reader feel your pain, but you don't want to relive the experience itself.

Writing is hard.

And it is not always safe.

Writing brings back people you haven't thought about for years.

Writing coaxes out your family, all of the friends you're ever had, every person you have met, and every experience you have had in your whole life.

And when the writing is over, you sit in a small room with your notebook in your lap, underneath the light of a lamp. All around you, filling the room, lined up in the shadows, taking up your light, are the images of all the things your writing brought out of your memory. These images join you in your dreams as you sleep, accompany you as you walk to class . . .

Writing a Dialogue

For the author of the excerpt above, writing out her reluctance to confront her past was an important step. After she had named her demons, so to speak, she went on to write a wonderful piece. But I suggested to the class that they need to do more than just write out their fears. I asked them to answer that negative voice and to make sure that they have the last word. This is an exercise that I recommend for you also.

Take out a piece of paper. You might even want to set aside a whole (little) notebook for this exercise. Now write a dialogue between these two selves: your good angel, who tells you you have an important story to tell, and your bad angel, who insists on the opposite. During the Renaissance, many people wrote dialogues between "self" and "soul," in which their better, spiritual side struggled with their more worldly or doubtful or disabling side. Their impulse may have been mostly religious, but such a dialogue can be an important exercise and resource for any writer living in any century. Here is an example of the dialogue I once wrote between myself and my inner voices:

SELF	CENSOR
I have an important story to tell.	No you don't. It's too late to write. You are too old, too much time has gone by and besides you didn't keep many records.
So what? The memories must be there somewhere.	Yes, but when you write them they come out sounding so flat and dry.
Well then, my imagination can step into the breach, and I can make up what I don't remember.	Your seventh grade teacher told you you have no imagination.
You've got to be kidding! Why should I listen to my seventh grade teacher at this point in my life?	Okay, okay. You win this time around. But remember you just don't have time to write.
I can find an hour a day.	Maybe . . . but your writing is so disorganized.
That's because it's rich. I haven't yet found the shape of the story. Give me time.	All right. I'll shut up for now.

When you write such a dialogue, it is important that you make sure you (your better self) has the last word. When you are finished, close that notebook and put it on a high shelf. Your censor has had a chance to speak and has been listened to seriously. He or she has been given a place, but now can be firmly told to shut up.

Later, if this voice insists again on intruding into your writing time, take the notebook out and write another dialogue. Again, be honest. Admit all your doubts and fears, but then put them aside—on a high shelf, in another room, in a drawer or a closet, some place where you can imagine those voices contained.

Sometimes we have to voice our doubts and fears (and our sorrows) before moving on. I found out the hard way that if I didn't let these voices speak in my head, they kept popping up anyway. Paradoxically, it was only by allowing them to speak that I could shut them up.

I have a friend, an artist, who was refused tenure, but who responded in a wonderfully creative and healthy way. She went to the local five-and-dime and bought all their little ceramic angels. She brought them home and painted them with little tatooes and tears and called them the tatooed angels who bring bad news. She did this in the kitchen, while she talked on the phone to her friends and family. After a couple of weeks, all the bad news had been expressed and acknowledged and she was ready to go on and paint some angels of good fortune.

She was able to move on from that place of grief and disappointment by first acknowledging it and expressing it creatively. You might look for your own little creative rituals, anything that helps you through the hard times of doubt and uncertainty, so that you can go back to writing.

Finding a Place of Safety

Writing a dialogue is one way to silence those voices that might get in your way. Another way is to find a place of safety where you can write free of interruptions. My students often talk about needing a room to themselves when they write; they can't just sit in the computer lab and write a personal narrative.

A friend of mine, who was raped at the age of twenty, wanted for years afterward to write about the experience. She never felt safe enough to do so until many years after the event when she asked her husband to sit across the room from her, not talking to her but reading the newspaper. Only then was she able to write. Another friend told me she had to lie flat on the floor and feel the hard solidness of the world, as she began to write.

It may not be as difficult for you to start to write,

but in any case finding a place of safety and quiet away from interruptions might be necessary.

EXERCISES

(1) Write a dialogue with those voices in your head that tell you you cannot write. In this dialogue, name your fears as accurately as you can (don't be ashamed to name them even if they seem very silly). Be sure to give yourself (not your negative voices) the last word.

(2) Keep a separate notebook for your negative internal voices. Give them a chance to express themselves, but when they are finished close the notebook and put it away. Keep a separate notebook for your real writing. Treat that other negative self respectfully, but then put him or her firmly back in place.

"SPOTS OF TIME"
Learning to Remember

MEMORY IS ESSENTIAL TO THE MEMOIR. I need hardly remind you that you must remember past events in order to tell them, or that when you start to write you might feel discouraged because of what you have forgotten. Be reassured, however, that *any* writer who sets out to write a first-person narrative is likely to run across problems with memory—too many trivial memories, too few vivid memories, family lies substituting for memory, merged memories, and the like.

As you will see in this chapter, however, these problems are not necessarily impediments to writing; with a little work they can become rich resources for telling a complex story. How we remember, what we forget, what preoccupies us about our past, which memories we avoid, which ones we obsessively retell —all of this can be the stuff of memoir writing. In other words, memory itself, in all its richness and in its deceptiveness (even including what we don't remember), can be a subject of memoir.

In this chapter, I will identify problems we commonly experience with memory, then discuss ways around these problems. You will see how writers of memoir often draw on single small images to generate whole passages. They frequently reflect on the process of remembering (or forgetting) in itself as an important resource for telling the story. I hope this chapter will help you not just to trust available memories, but also to value "thinking small," to realize that the memories we keep are tremendously important precisely because they are the ones we have retained. The exercises at the end of this chapter spell out strategies for "learning to remember" fruitfully.

Making Lists

I have a friend who, in her sixties, started trying to reconstruct early experiences which she had forgotten. She was very frustrated by what she did not remember, so I suggested she write a list of what she did remember, and also a list of what she did not remember. Not so surprisingly, she began to remember much more as a result of writing these two lists. Here is some of what she did remember:

Steering the car while grandpa drove; going into the ditch.
Dressing up the cat; putting her in the carriage.
Sunday school in a family of agnostics.
My mother; temper; doing nails and hair.
My mother's attempted suicide.

Here is some of what she did not remember:

How old was my Grandmother when she died? Was she buried? If, so where?
What year did Grandpa take up with his mistress?
When was I taken from my mother? Who picked me up? What was said?

Even a cursory look at these two lists reveals not only rich subject matter, but some clues as to how the story might be told. After working on several passages and feeling a lot of frustration over her loss of memory, my friend decided to start with the scene in which, at the age of eleven, she was taken from her mother and sent alone on a train to live with other relatives. This scene provided her with a way into the story. It was a decisive moment of departure, a rupture from the past, and it introduced a pause in time, the time on the train when the child is suspended between worlds. This scene gave a starting point from which the writer could explore the past and ask specifically how the child happened to be on the train in the first place.

Mostly, I wanted to suggest to my friend that she write about what she didn't know, as well as what she did remember. She didn't have to remember everything, or confirm everything through letters and other documents. The gaps and losses in memory are clues to family silences around important secrets, and to why certain decisions were made. They tell us something about why the child lost or erased certain memories. For example, I told my friend she might explore why she remembers her mother's attempted suicide, but not who picked her up on the other side of the country when she was sent away from her mother.

What we forget as well as what we remember can be a rich resource for the memoir writer. It is important that you identify and explore those gaps or silences in your own history. Allow yourself to speculate about what you don't know, and don't remember. A later chapter will help you to find and use tangible resources for writing besides memory—those letters, deeds, wills, divorce documents, medical records, and other documents which can supplement lost or flawed memories. For now, rather than worrying about gaps and silences, realize they are actually vital to the story.

Thinking Small

In a piece on memory and the imagination, Patricia Hampl reminds us that "We only store memories of value." It doesn't matter how small your memories are; they can become a rich resource for your writing. Forget about grand schemes for now, and find a memory that is little, but that you keep going back to. As you explore that memory, search for one or two or three sharp details. You might well discover that these details are enough to get you started writing.

Here is the way Harry Crews, in *A Childhood: The Biography of a Place*, tells the story of his first memory. Notice in this passage that he includes a few sharp sensual memories; he also admits what he did not know at the time when he experienced this moment.

It has always seemed to me that I was not so much born into this life as awakened to it. I remember very distinctly the awakening and the morning it happened. It was my first glimpse of myself, and all that I know now—the stories, and everything conjured up by them . . . I obviously knew none of then, particularly anything about my real daddy, whom I was not to hear of until I was nearly six years old, not his name, not even that he was my daddy. Or if I did hear of him, I have no memory of it.

I awoke in the middle of the morning in early

summer from the place I'd been sleeping in the
curving roots of a giant oak tree in front of a large
white house. . . . At my feet was a white dog whose
name was Sam. I looked at the dog and at the house
and at the red gown with little pearl-colored buttons
I was wearing, and I knew that the gown had been
made for me by my Grandma Hazelton and that the
dog belonged to me. He went everywhere I went,
and he always took precious care of me. (Quoted
on pages 1 and 2 of Dillard and Conley, *Modern
American Memoirs*)

Notice how Crews thinks small: the dog, the red gown
with the little pearl-colored buttons, the house, the
tree, these details are vivid enough to evoke a scene
of awakening. In fact, the scene follows his own se-
quential looking first at one object then another: "I
looked at the dog and at the house . . ." But by telling
us what he didn't know, he alerts us to a mystery, something that might well generate a narrative
to follow. In doing this, Crews separates the child-
protagonist of four as he appears in this narrative
from himself as an older writer, or as the narrative
voice who tells us what he did not know as a young
child. (This kind of separation of voices will be discussed in a later chapter.)

Writing About What You Don't Remember

Most writers starting out (myself included) believe that we must remember accurately and well and then transcribe our memories. We believe vivid recall is absolutely essential to good writing. But, as I hope you are beginning to see, this isn't really true. Vivian Gornick is another writer who skillfully inserts what she didn't know into a passage telling us what she does remember. You can see from the following excerpt from her book *Fierce Attachments* that exploring a vague memory, even a memory later identified as false or partial, can give rise to vivid writing:

I lived in that tenement between the ages of six and twenty-one. There were twenty apartments, four to a floor, and all I remember is a building full of women. I hardly remember the men at all. They were everywhere, of course—husbands, fathers, brothers—but I remember only the women. And I remember them all crude like Mrs. Drucker or fierce like my mother. They never spoke as though they knew who they were, understood the bargain they had struck with life, but they often acted as though they knew . . . There would be years of apparent calm, then suddenly an outbreak of panic and wildness: two or three lives scarred (perhaps ruined), and the turmoil would subside. Once again: sullen quiet, erotic torpor, the ordinariness of daily denial. And I—the girl growing in their midst, being

33

made in their image—I absorbed them as I would chloroform on a cloth laid against my face. It has taken me thirty years to understand how much of them I understood. (Pages 3–4)

Once again we are being set up for a revelation. The fact that the author does not know or remember certain things only enriches the narrative. And again the writer separates her wise, knowing, narrator voice from the girl-protagonist who merely absorbs all this chaos as though breathing it in. Notice how much she conveys by using words like "all I remember," "I hardly remember," "I remember only," or "It has taken me thirty years to understand." She doesn't pretend to a knowledge she doesn't have, but she skillfully uses what she does know.

Using All the Senses to Evoke Memories

Now, let's suppose you have written a list of what you don't remember, as well as a list of the memories you have retained. Perhaps you have even started to explore the loss of memory but still feel you are getting nowhere. Sometimes we don't remember at all because we lack the language for establishing a memory. Such can be the case with our earliest experiences, and with traumatic experiences that lie outside our frame of reference, our worldview, or our language. We may be too young to have mastered enough language skills for laying down a memory in the first place, but recent research on post-traumatic stress syndrome and on repressed memories indicates that such memory losses may occur at any time in our lives. Some experiences seem so awful that we simply have no words for them. Instead, we store such memories as sense impressions (sound, sight, smell) or viscerally as bodily sensations such as the feeling of falling or of being smothered.

Such impressions can be very useful to the writer of memoir. The memories themselves might be there just below the surface, ready to be tapped. Trying to reconstruct a scene through sight, smell, sound, or sensation can be an evocative way of writing, even if you do not remember a scene exactly as it happened.

In her book *Trauma and Recovery*, Judith Herman gives psychological insight into the loss and recovery of memory, which can be very helpful to the writer as well as the patient. Herman reminds us that "Traumatic memory is . . . wordless and static." (Page 173) Such memories might seem to be like a series of still snapshots; they don't progress or develop in time and the images might be disconnected from feelings. Extreme trauma, she reminds us, such as that of warfare or of sexual assault, might be stored in this way, rather than in readily recalled language-based memories.

Any experience of radical cultural dislocation can involve such memory loss or absence. Moving from one country to another, one language to another, es-

35

pecially if it happens at a crucial moment in a child's development, can have this effect. Immigrant narratives, as well as certain other cross-cultural writings, frequently mention this kind of loss. The writers recount more than the loss of a home or a country; even the sense of a dependable outside reality is lost, as well as the inner narrative which each of us uses to construct a "self." *Lost in Translation*, Eva Hoffman's account of moving from Poland to Canada at the age of thirteen, is a brilliant example of such a narrative. When she goes to bed at night in Vancouver, Eva can no longer name her experiences; she tries out different adjectives and nouns for the people she has met during the day, but finds that there are simply no suitable words available in her consciousness. She has lost her inner voice.

Sometimes in a class I will ask my students to make a list of images or single words and phrases, whatever comes to their minds, as they attempt to recall an experience. If certain memories (and not just traumatic ones) are stored mostly in sense impressions, then I tell them to use what they've got. But I ask my students to write lists for another reason as well. I want them to turn off the editorial mind that wants to sort and shape, to order and evaluate and interpret experience. At the beginning, simply getting an event down on paper is far more important. At times it is useful to write of the experience with the perspective of one sense only, sight or sound or taste or smell, for example. Or you might try to evoke each of these senses.

A therapist who works with combat veterans describes her approach to recovery through telling in this way: "We ask them to reel it off in great detail, as though they are watching a movie, and with all the senses included. We ask them what they are seeing, what they are hearing, what they are smelling, what they are feeling. . . ." (Herman, page 177) You could do the same: just start with what you've got, no matter how fragmentary and inchoate it may seem.

Here is how the writer Natalie Kusz recounts the traumatic experience of being anesthetized for surgery following an attack by sled dogs in her book *Road Song*. Kusz was a young child when this happened, and all she had to draw on for writing about it later were some very basic sense impressions. The following passage, however, shows how rich these fragmentary impressions are:

There is a certain sound in the ears, like the crashing of rapids between stone walls, and a certain aluminum taste in the throat—familiar spirits who enter the moment before one succumbs to anesthesia. For that long instant, all of the senses are heightened—voices in the air grow louder, lights overhead brighter—and it always seemed to me that the moment before death must be quite like this, that in the body's final second it must enlarge outside itself to capture as much as the senses can hold, enveloping and drawing them quickly within, before the spirit leaves, and with it all awareness. It was only after being anesthetized many times that I learned not to fight it, not to claw ineffectually against unconsciousness and wake convulsing on the other side, but instead to relax into it, to close my eyes and lean backward into the operating table, further and further, as if the earth would open and my body would tumble into it whole, shoulders first. In the middle of it all, I would twitch—like a dreamer falling from a cliff—but this was no great nuisance, and was small cost for the lung-deep relief of abandoning desperation, of relinquishing hold on that which I did not control in the first place. (Pages 104–105)

Notice how, in this passage, Kusz draws on the sense of hearing ("the crashing of rapids between stone walls"), taste ("a certain aluminum taste in the throat"), proprioception, or the sense of the body in space ("lean backward into the operating table, further and further, as if the earth would open and my body would tumble into it whole, shoulders first," "I would twitch like a dreamer falling from a cliff."). These are the simple visceral experiences of being anesthetized. The interpretation of the experience obviously comes to her later as the adult reflects on what the experience might mean ("it always seemed to me that the moment before death must be quite like this").

Turning a Vague Memory Into a Vivid Moment

Sometimes the problem isn't loss of memory, but *too many* memories. At times, when we start to write we have the feeling that we have simply remembered too many extraneous details, and the task we have before us as writers is to sort through the mass of details to get to the one core image which will speak to the reader. Paradoxically, psychologists tell us that we need to forget in order to remember. The mind seems to be so constituted that each day, mostly by way of dreams, we must sort through the mountain of details which makes up our daily experience in order to hang on to those few things worth remembering. And to do this, we must forget the rest.

When I started to write, I was appalled by how much I had forgotten. It seemed that whole years had been wiped out of my life. If I did recall events, it was through what I call "habitual" memory. I retained merged memories of similar events that happened over and over again, but not single vivid moments. And this kind of generic memory, I felt, was not very useful in writing. I wanted each individual moment.

All my memories were merged, jumbled together. I couldn't pick out the single, striking image that would capture a reader's attention. It was a long time before I began to realize that a generic memory can become a particular one; it can be reexperienced through the writing itself so that the vague memory of repeated events can become the single compelling memory which stands for all the others.

Annie Dillard, in a wonderful image, observes that writers "cannibalize" their memories and warns us that if we want to preserve our memories as memories, we had better not write. She notes how vivid the written-out "made-up" memory becomes; it actually supplants the real memory and as such is experienced more vividly than the memory itself.

At first I was troubled by the experience of supplanting memory by writing. I felt I was being dishonest when I embellished my poor memories so that they became something entirely new, "made-up," in fact. Now I am not so worried about this process; I think of it as a natural part of writing. Here is one such memory of mine, experienced many times and not remembered as a single time, but told now as a single event so that it stands for all that is forgotten:

I am standing in front of the theater marquee in our small town. It is seven o'clock in the evening and the lights are flickering rapidly. I am holding the hand of a beautiful two-year-old boy, my son, who stands entranced by the lights, fixated, hardly moving. Each night at seven he insists on coming to watch them, and I bring him willingly, cheerfully explaining to our friends as they enter the theater why I am there, how much he loves these lights. At first I see nothing strange in this. Paul loves lights.

He turns them off and on for hours each day. He
knows where every light switch is in our house and
the houses of our friends and in many of the stores
downtown. His world is lights and light switches.
(Page 1)

This is the first paragraph of *News From the Border*,
my account of my son's autism and of all of our lives
"under the aspect of autism." I needed to find some
concrete way to introduce the reader to autism in the
young child, while simultaneously showing my own
ignorance of it at that time. The experience of watching the flickering lights at the movie theater across
the street from our house became the single image
which I hoped would bear the burden of so much
else. Paul's singleminded focus on lights, his fascination with what for other children would only be a
passing interest, my willingness to share with him his
pleasure in something so simple, and my ignorance
and innocence about what his fascination might
mean—I tried to suggest all of this in my brief rec-
ollection. Later in the book the reader learns how to
interpret this image of Paul and the lights and begins to understand that autistic children have sensory
dysfunctions which are expressed in odd repetitive
behaviors. At the beginning I just wanted to transform my "flawed" memories into a single memorable
image.

Without really knowing it, I was finding a "spot of

time," the poet Wordsworth's name for such moments of awareness, or rather for images which *precede*
awareness. Wordsworth identified these moments as
mostly coming from childhood, but whether they
come from the child's or the adult's experience, these
memories "nourish" and "invisibly repair" the mind.
For the writer, they are moments of grace that fuse
feeling with incident in such a way that those moments bear the burden of meaning for much else—
and it is usually only later that we realize this.

In my case, the image of lights became a central
one for showing the alertness of a child who nevertheless failed to develop normally later. Here is another passage which uses that simple image:

> I remember another scene. Two years earlier. In the
> delivery room, we watch the first moments of this
> new baby. Taken up in a bundle of loose blankets,
> he is placed on the warming table. Crying, rolling
> vigorously from side to side, he kicks, breaks free of
> the folds of the fabric and opens his eyes. Most new-
> borns that I have seen are curled in on themselves,
> as if they need to fold themselves away from the
> onslaught of the world for fear it be seen too soon,
> too suddenly. Not this one. This baby seems to open
> his eyes to the full sense of things all at once. Eyes
> opened wide, he stops crying and stares at the lights
> on the ceiling. "He's a keeper," exclaims the at-
> tending nurse, and in my new mother's egotism, this
> seems like a wonderful omen. I think I have never

seen such sudden sense, such full, startled awareness, such awakening to the world. (Page 1)

As I continued to write, I found myself returning
over and over again to the image of lights—to a two-
year-old child fascinated by flickering lights, a new-
born noticing the light on the ceiling of the delivery
room, and then a year-old child trying to say his first
word ("ight"), and somehow failing. From such a wel-
ter of images and memories, I decided to focus on
that one image—light—as a way into the first year of
my child's life. Single images can be wonderful entry
points into our narratives.

As you start to write about a difficult past, consider
all these examples. You might simply write down the
sense impressions you have retained about an experience, as Kusz did in writing about the experience of
anesthesia. You might find a single image, as I did in
the flickering lights of a movie theater. Here are some
exercises to get you started.

EXERCISES

(1) Write about an experience using one sense
only.

(2) Write of the experience, drawing on each of
the senses (sight, sound, touch, smell, taste, proprioception or the sense of the body in space), but with-

43

out giving any commentary or interpretation of the experience.

(3) Choose one vague memory of something that happened over and over again. Retell this generic memory as if it happened just once. In telling it as a single, one-time memory, try to evoke the experience as a single vivid moment in time.

(4) List all the things you do not remember, such as a birth or a death, but which you know are important to your story. After making the list, chose one or two facts and explore them as important, although unremembered. You can introduce this material through interviews with family members or through letters. (Later chapters will tell you more about how to go about doing this.)

~ 3

"JUST MAKE IT UP,
THEN SEE IF IT IS TRUE"

Imagination Coming to the Aid of Memory

YOU CAN LEARN to trust even flawed memories; but what if you simply do not remember something you want to write about? What if you weren't present at an event which is, nevertheless, an important part of the story you want to tell? The discussion and exercises offered in this chapter build on those in the last chapter.

The title of this chapter comes from a comment Vivian Gornick made in a class I took with her at The Loft in Minneapolis. Gornick was responding to a student who complained that he simply could not remember an experience he needed to write about. "Well, just make it up," she said. "Then see if it is true."

Those words stayed with me far longer than I would have guessed at the time. I thought about them

45

again and again as I was struggling to finish my first book. Well, yes, I thought to myself, of course we have to make up a lot. If we can't remember the exact words someone said (and usually we don't) we have to fabricate. And there are so many other elements as well: the physical setting, what the characters looked like, maybe facts like the weather, the time of year. We may have forgotten any of these details, or perhaps we never knew them in the first place.

As I thought about Gornick's words, I kept wondering about her advice to "see if it is true." That's the catch, I thought. How does one decide which made-up moments are "real" and which are not? Of course, there are some touchstones. For example, you can ask yourself what behavior or gesture or words would be characteristic of someone you know? Or you might think about what didn't happen, but should have—by the logic of events. Occasionally, in creative nonfiction, you will need to make real events seem plausible by adding somewhat fictionalized passages leading up to those events. Or you may want to write about a past event which affected you deeply, but which you did not experience directly.

The best way to deal with such problems is to acknowledge them directly as problems and to involve your reader in your efforts to recreate an unknown or partly forgotten past. These problems can become rich resources for writing, because it is your reflections on what you cannot know and what you imagine to be true, your frustrations at not knowing more, and your willingness to actively engage the unknown which, finally, will give your narrative candor and power.

Think of stories from your past or from your family's past. Maybe there are some stories about which you know very little, but which continue to haunt you. Perhaps you think of your grandfather's unexplained desertion of his family long ago. Or you keep wondering about your mother's breakdown when she was a teenager; she has told you a little bit, but not very much, and you suspect that this experience might explain a lot of later events. Maybe you have heard the story of a family move and a change of job which has never quite been explained. Whatever the secrets are (the never-quite-told stories), they can be a powerful part of your ongoing narrative of yourself to yourself. You may often find yourself speculating about such stories, whether they are discussed in your family or not.

So what do you do if you are trying to write your own story and your life history involves some unknown stories from your past or your family's past? Do you just make it up by embellishing the few facts you do have? Do you search for documents, and write only what is completely verifiable (from legal records, family correspondence, etc.)?

There isn't any one right way to solve this dilemma, no template you can apply to your own writing which will always work in every case. Instead, as you will see, there are a range of options.

How to Use a Little Knowledge

Sometimes the problem is that you know a little bit, but not very much, about a powerful family story. Let's say this is something which happened in the past, but which you can't uncover by asking more questions or searching for documents. You know a few facts, you wish desperately that you knew more, but you can't ask (your mother, your brother, your aunt, your friend), for whatever reason.

This is a case where invention might be openly acknowledged and might, furthermore, be a necessary part of the memoir writer's response to the unknown. Maxine Hong Kingston's *The Woman Warrior* is one of the most important and influential modern memoirs we have; yet it is highly fictionalized. In fact, fiction-making is a necessary part of this book precisely because it is a memoir and not a novel. I know this sounds paradoxical, yet it is the imaginative response to stories from the past (the protagonist's mother's stories from old China) and to troubling memories from a more recent time which make this book what it is. Because the author knows so little about some things, she must make up a lot.

This is a book well worth reading closely, especially the short first chapter in which the protagonist is told a story by her mother about her pregnant aunt who drowned herself in the family well. Very little is known about that aunt; furthermore, even to mention the fact of her existence is to break a powerful family taboo. And yet Kingston is, of course, powerfully drawn to this forbidden story told by her mother as a cautionary tale: "Now that you have started to menstruate, what happened to her could happen to you. Don't humiliate us." She can't help but speculate about this aunt, "No Name Woman."

Kingston wonders if the aunt may have been a victim of rape or seduction. She first considers the possibility of forced "consent," spinning out a number of possible scenarios to explain why her aunt got pregnant at a time when her husband was abroad. Then she speculates that she might have been the victim of her own vanity: "She plied her secret comb. And sure enough she cursed the year, the family, the village, and herself." Or she may have been "Unusually beloved, the precious only daughter, spoiled and mirror gazing because of the affection the family lavished on her." Kingston goes on to speculate about who the man was; about how the man and the other villagers sought revenge on her for becoming pregnant. And so forth.

Such stories, precisely because so little is known, are rich material for the memoirist: "Unless I see her life branching into mine, she gives me no ancestral help," Kingston tells us. The "No Name Woman"

must be reimagined before Kingston can go on to tell
"real" facts about her own life and history, and that
is why she begins her own personal narrative with
what she doesn't know about her family's past.

As an exercise for yourself, take a story about
which you have just a few facts. Speculate as Kingston
does; take some of these tag phrases, these invitations
to reflection and speculation, and complete them:

I only know that . . .
Perhaps this is what happened . . .
She/He must have thought this . . .
I have not been told all of this story because . . .
Nobody knows why . . .
I think he/she did this because . . .

One of my students found herself very preoccupied with the story of her mother's abuse by her
grandfather. My student happened to overhear this
story when, as a young child, she was hiding in the
closet of an older sister's room. She overheard her
two older sisters talking about the abuse, but because
she felt guilty about hearing the story by eavesdropping, she thought she could not ask them, or her
mother, to tell her more.

The story about eavesdropping became the entry
point into the student's narrative about being the
third daughter in her family. Though she decided not
to begin the piece with this memory, it helped her to

understand her position in the family. She wrote and rewrote the scene until she got sick of it, but after that she was able to go on with the rest of her narrative. Her intense preoccupation with this secret, precisely because it was a secret known by everyone but not "officially" known by her, compelled her to write about it first. Later she went on to write about herself as the beloved third child in the family, someone who was always thought of as the "baby" and protected from certain painful stories.

Using a Place to Imagine the Past

In the following sections, I will quote from two contemporary Irish writers, Eavan Boland and Sebastian Barry. Like Kingston, they also write about a past they do not know directly, yet both end up "witnessing" to that past. Their pieces, however, are somewhat different from Kingston's. Boland and Barry invite us into a physical scene where an event took place. By using scenes which they know well (Dublin streets, an old house), both of them lead us imaginatively into the past.

In her book *Object Lessons*, Boland writes about her grandmother, who died during childbirth in the National Maternity Hospital in Dublin. She has learned only a few facts about her grandmother's life from her mother, yet she finds herself returning again and again to the last scenes of her life outside the hospital.

51

In the early days of October, in the year 1909, a woman entered a Dublin hospital, near the center of the city. The building is still there. If you approach from the south, with the Dublin hills behind you, and look down a tunnel of grace made by the houses of Fitzwilliam and Merrion squares, your view will end abruptly in this: the National Maternity Hospital, red brick and out of character, blocking the vista . . .

October is a beautiful month in the city. If you turn around and go back towards the hills, away from the hospital, the roads are narrow and gracious above the canal. The woman who entered the hospital may have passed them as she made her way to it. If, for instance, she drove around Stephen's Green, having arrived on the late-morning train from Drogheda, she may also have noticed a trick of light peculiar to that time of year: In the dark corridor of Lower Leeson Street, sunlight cuts the houses in half. Halfway up the brick the reflection of the houses opposite builds another street: chimneys, roofs, gutters made of unglittering shadow.

She may not have come that way. She might have traveled down the unglamorous back streets that lead more directly to the hospital. Fenian Street. Hogan Place. Past the mills. Past the Dodder River on its way to the Liffey. Up the slight gradient which would still, in that year, be cobbled. The prewinter chill, which can be felt on some October mornings, could have struck extra music out of the horses' hooves.

It is not a long drive. But whatever she saw that morning, it is lost. Whatever that journey yielded— the child with a hoop who never existed, the woman with the red hat I am now inventing—they were her last glimpses of the outside world.

~ ~ ~

This is the way we make the past. This is the way I will make it here. Listening for hooves. Glimpsing the red hat which was never there in the first place. Giving eyesight and evidence to a woman we never knew and cannot now recover. And for all our violations, the past waits for us. The road from the train to the hospital opens out over and over again, vacant and glittering, offering shadows and hats and hoops. Again and again I visit it and reinvent it. But the woman who actually traveled it had no such license. Hers was a real journey. She did not come back. On October 10 she died in the National Maternity Hospital. She was thirty-one years of age. She was my grandmother. (Pages 3–5)

Notice that Boland doesn't tell us this is her grandmother until the very end of the passage. Instead she deliberately reconstructs the scene which "the woman" might have traveled through, mentioning the October chill, a seasonal trick of the light, a glimpse of a woman in a red hat, a child with a hoop. Boland does not pretend omniscience but rather insists on the deliberateness of her own imaginative reconstruction ("the child with a hoop who never existed, the woman with a red hat I am now inventing . . ."). She admits that she cannot ever really know what her grandmother saw and felt that day which was to be the last day of her life in the outside world. Restraining any impulse to "know" what cannot be known, she instead invites the reader on her imaginative journey ("If you approach from the south . . . ," "If you turn around and go back to the hills . . .").

This passage from *Object Lessons* is as much a meditation on history and the imagination, a reflection on the "license" allowed the memoir writer, as it is a factual account. The extraordinary power of this passage comes from the imaginative reconstruction around the edges of those few known events. The writer's preoccupation with this largely unknown past, her understanding that to write about it she must in a sense violate it, her recognition that her grandmother "had no such license" to tell her own story: all of these things inform the passage, and make it much more than a mere recitation of events would have been.

This passage demonstrates how the imagination can come to the aid of memory, and how a piece of writing can be more powerful precisely because so little is known. As an exercise for your own writing, try completing the following sentence fragments:

When I return to that place where she/he was . . .
The weather at that time of year would have
been . . .
Maybe she saw . . .
Maybe he traveled by a different road . . .

If you wish, write a speculative passage about what
a place means to you, or what a past event means to
you at this moment in time. Place can be powerfully
evocative. If we know that an event happened in a
particular place, but we know little about feelings,
motivations or events leading up to that moment in
the past, we can write about the place instead, as Boland did.

Enacting a Discovery

The following excerpt from Sebastian Barry's "Note
From the Dead," included in the anthology *Dublines*,
is similar to Boland's piece in that the writer here is
also tentative; he too hypothesizes a past which cannot be known directly. But in this case the writing
enacts a *discovery* of a message from the past. It is the
writer's presence in the scene of his discovery which
makes this piece so compelling.

One evening in 1974, I took a stroll through the old
house in Mountjoy Square where I was living in a

flat, poking into dead rooms, toeing odds and ends of boxes and drawers. You could walk a big dog in a place like that and count it exercised. No one else was in; or maybe the scholar who lived upstairs was picking over some page of Joyce above, silent and mesmerized. And I felt that sense of other lives, I saw clearly, separately, the old brownness of the paint that was no longer paint in the halls, but a ghost, a coffin-coloured remnant of true paint. I heard the steps, the countless steps, the privacy of those roomkeepers going out for whatever private purchases into the greater city.

Dark winter as always, the late day full of gloom outside the windows, every object I saw beginning to speak its story, to clamour to be heard, to explain, to detail disaster and the victory of sudden joys. Each old table had been picked and purchased new once, pennies pinched to have it, each door had been opened and shut a million times . . .

The lower landing was readying up for revelation, for a tiny information to me, a preparation, a hint at the very stuff of life . . . I wandered into the most battered room of the house where there wasn't even a frame in the window, only a jagged sheet of thick plastic over the hole, and the night wind icing in, and the streetlamps forward and blunt in the debris.

Here was a little tin box. I prised it open with a nail and took out a piece of old blue writing paper, the sort I used to write to my father on when he was away in London, old blue paper folded a few times

into a small irregular shape. It had the dirt outside
of something often handled but less often unfolded,
as if it had been taken from spot to spot, extracted
from book to niche to tin, over the span of a life.
So settled in its folds it was almost difficult to
open it.

The surface inside looked quite crisp and new, as
if it had just been written on, and the writing was in
fresh pencil. The paper spoke, you could hear its
voice, in the list of names and the few bleak
sentences:

In this room on the night of January
the 2nd the coldest night of the year
we went to bed all hale, and awoke to
find three of our number dead, Jamie
(Brown) aged 7 Mary and Christie Finlay,
3 months, 11 years from suffocation.
And the rest not much better.

Under this, there was an entry in a different hand,
or the same hand at a different time, a tireder hand
perhaps, listing two others, two of the old ones, who
died

we suppose from the late effects of the same
cause.

I, Jane Finlay, mother, write this down, the
names of our loved ones. We must never forget
this. (Pages 299–300)

This discovery is, of course, stunning to the writer.
But the power of its presentation to us is partly de-

pendent on the language of the writer of the note, Jane Finlay. Her simple words would affect anyone reading her little message. Yet the scene might have lost its power if Barry had come upon these words too soon. They must be approached, and approached very slowly, as he moves through those rooms where he lives only temporarily.

Somewhat like Boland, he reflects on his discovery, and he takes us with him; as readers, we must of necessity follow him emotionally:

What was to be done with such a discovery? What did it mean? When I was long gone out of that house I used to think of that room, think of that family sleeping there in the great privacy, the secrecy of poverty, and that coldest night of the year, and that woman of the elegant words writing down the record of the event . . .

I suppose I was the first person to read that piece of notepaper since the last hand belonging to it had passed away from the world so thoroughly that even it, a precious document, an heirloom, a history, had not been safekept. It had lain in its tin box for decades in a room of rubble . . .

I'm sure I took it with me, stuffed it in my jacket. I'm sure I took it with me out of that room and I'm equally sure I lost it. Not in safe hands! Or at best it sits among old papers of mine in some old box in my mother's house, waiting for a fresh reader, a second hearer, a better seer. I hope Jane Finlay died a

nicer death than her people did that night, when it
got so cold, and they stopped up the window with
rags, that fine old Georgian window, and minute by
minute their lungs used up the precious air, and
warm enough they died, and cold she awoke, to rise,
and shake her dead, and write her note.

   (quoted on pages 299–301 of Donovan & Kennelly, *Dublines*)

Once again, the writer uses his imagination to
come to the aid of memory or historical record. The
discovery itself becomes important here, for Barry
comprehends the importance of his find. And
even though this piece bears powerful witness to a
tragedy largely unknown, he also feels he tells the
story inadequately. But, oddly, it is his feeling of inadequacy which makes this piece so affecting. We
know instinctively that any relation of this story would
be insufficient. He writes as the memoirist writes, fully
aware of the limitations of his own telling, but at the
same time fully honest about the effects of his discovery.

As you think about this passage, you might write
something similar. Perhaps you have discovered a letter from the past, or you have found a message
scrawled on a wall by a child who lived in your home
long ago, or you heard the story of an event which
happened in your neighborhood long before you
moved in. Try writing out your approach to this bit

of information the way Barry does, placing the discovery within the context of its significance to you as the finder. You might complete statements such as these:

> When I found the letter, it was just the wrong time of my life for such a discovery . . . (Or it was just the right time . . .)
> I often wonder what they thought as they looked out this window . . .
> I lost that piece of paper and now I think that . . .

Imagining a Scene Where You Were Not Present

Both Boland and Barry are preoccupied with events they didn't directly experience. Here is another example of such a telling, but with a difference: this time the writer actually imagines herself into the mind and feelings of her subject. But in doing so, this writer is also careful to remind us that she is, in fact, merely imagining what cannot be known directly. This is a passage from one of my students in a college writing class, a student who told me at the beginning of the term that she wanted to write about the suicide of a high school acquaintance. She hadn't known this other student very well, yet the dead girl appeared in her dreams over and over again. Not surprisingly, something about that death continued to preoccupy

my student, but it was a while before she realized that
she could write about what she hadn't witnessed, that
she could make it up, then see if it was true. Here is
how she told the story of the girl's death:

What happened that day? I am compelled by my
wonder, by my need for answers to re-enact the
scene over and over in my head.

She's sitting at the coffee table balancing her
checkbook. Balancing her life and something
doesn't fit. Nothing ever fits. The sadness holds the
teeter-totter at one end. No matter what she puts on
the other side, there is no balance.

Her parents are in the kitchen. They are fighting
again. This time it's serious. Her mother has had
enough of the disrespect, of being ignored, of the
lies, and the cheating. Her father flips through the
newspaper as if she isn't even there. "I'm leaving!
Do you hear me? Leaving!" Her father glances up
as if to say "Don't forget to close the door behind
you." It seems that nothing will stop her this time.
Nothing?

It's a beautiful day in early February. It seems out
of place in the middle of winter. But everyone is
thankful for the birdcalls and puddles at the curb.
I remember it had been especially cold up until this
day. The sun is heating up the room where she sits,
and together with the shouting the temperature becomes unbearable.

So silently, calmly she puts down her pen

and walks to her parents' bedroom. It's the largest, safest room in the house. She remembers how she tried on her mother's clothes and smelled her father's cologne. The nights she spent in their bed when the lightning flashed and the thunder boomed. Today it's the sun that sends her to this refuge.

She must have hesitated. This I believe. She must have fumbled. Grabbed the door to turn away, made a noise to make someone stop her. Yet, no one listened. So she goes to the drawer that's haunted her life of late. Digging around for the cold steel. She begins to cry or tremble or scream. No. They would have heard this. There is no noise, no motion, no emotion. To do what she did you remain stoic; you hold yourself together for the most emphatic moment of your life. Deciding, I guess, would be the hard part. The rest is easy.

She clutches the black machine. The gun that will take her life. Kill her. Dead. But it's not this harsh today. The sun coming in the window now lights up the white room. It's so bright that she shades her eyes from the glare.

White, everywhere.

The small black object becomes the center of her focus as the only item in the room that she can look at. The only item in the room that doesn't mock her with its pure whiteness. Just what everyone thought she was.

My imagination fails here. I cannot recreate suicide. The gun to her head or in her mouth. The last deep breath, the pulling of the trigger, the deafening blast . . .

Kids play on the street outside her house. I used to ride my bike through this neighborhood as a child admiring the large houses. Thinking that one day I'd have a house just like this one or that one. In a neighborhood like this kids always play on the street. There's always laughter and childish taunting.

The sound that silences. Time stops and the children are gone as if they'd never been playing in the street, riding their bikes through the neighborhood. Inside, the white walls are stained red. Pureness tainted. What they'd forgotten was the golden, red hair. Her defining aspect in the middle of whiteness. She wasn't perfect, she had color and depth and sorrow. No one ever knew what her red hair meant and now it's touched every part of the room . . .

There are some things the writer knew about that day. She knew it had been cold, but that day in February was unexpectedly sunny and warm. Perhaps she knew what the bedroom looked like—that it was the largest and whitest room in the house. She knew the girl had red hair. And that she killed herself with a gun, which had been kept in a bedside drawer.

She probably didn't know that her friend had been trying to balance her checkbook or that her parents were fighting in the kitchen or that they often fought. She may have known these things, but even if she did not, they seem to fit with this imagined scene. The neighborhood she does know, the big houses that she, the writer, had often envied. Ironically, it is a large, safe neighborhood where children are often outside playing in the streets.

Notice also how she introduces herself into the scene, ("I am compelled by my wonder"), and then later pauses and qualifies ("She must have hesitated. This I believe."). And later still: "My imagination fails here. I cannot recreate suicide." Part of the power of this scene, in fact, comes precisely because it is told from the perspective of someone who was not there yet who was deeply affected by the event. This is first-person witnessing of a particular kind which demonstrates one of the peculiar advantages of memoir writing. We can't help but believe the writer, partly because she dares to recreate an experience in her imagination, and perhaps even more because she dares to testify to a terrible "truth" (a suicide) which can *only* be imagined.

Making Up Scenes to Introduce a Memory

There are other writing problems where the imagination can come to the aid of memory, where in fact it is only the imagination which can help us out. Sometimes we need to bring together several small memories to create a whole scene, and sometimes this involves making up part of the story as a kind of "glue" to hold together the events which we know happened. The resulting piece can become a seamless fabric of "real" and "made up" moments, and the reader may not even know where one leaves off and the other begins.

The following is from a chapter in my book *News from the Border* about living in London the year my son was three. This was before we knew he was autistic, and I needed to find a way to convey my confusion and his distress. I needed to show Paul's specific behaviors which would eventually point the way to the diagnosis of autism, but I had to be careful not to overinterpret those early times or to give away what I would later learn. I needed to keep the reader in a kind of suspense, and to take the reader along with me as I tried to understand what was going on with my son.

In working through all this, I chose an actual scene and then decided to lead up to it with a made-up scene. The imagined scene, however, is something that might well have happened. This is the scene which actually happened:

> Then, taking Paul by one hand and pulling the cart behind me with the other, I started for the crosswalk, the zebra crossing. But he wasn't ready to be cooperative. He lagged behind me, so that I had to drag him into the street as soon as I saw the crossing

light. Then the light changed just as we were halfway across. I looked up and saw a large lorry bearing down on us. I knew the driver had time to brake, but he probably expected us to cross and he slowed down only slightly.

I took all this in in a flash. Abruptly Paul broke free of my hand and lay down in the middle of the street. The truck stopped, but only just in time, and now cars were screeching to a stop and honking. I tried to pull Paul up and also hang on to my cart, which was starting to roll away from me. I couldn't do both. And then, there at my elbow was an old woman, so small that she hardly came up to my shoulder.

"Here, love, let me help you." She took the cart, and I bent to pick up Paul and carry him across the street.

At the other side, I put him down, and through my tears turned to thank her.

She smiled, the sweetest smile I had seen in weeks, and reached out to pat my arm. "That's all right, dear. I have a retarded son, too. I know what it's like. I remember."

And then she was gone and I stood staring. "Retarded?" But Paul's not retarded.

Or was he?

All the rest of the way home, the old woman's words rang in my ears. She had appeared at my shoulder like an angel of mercy, yet she had said those awful words, those words meant to comfort but which had hurt so terribly. (Page 37)

It was really true that Paul had lain in the middle of a busy London street and an old woman had stopped to help me and then spoken those words. The point about this scene for me later as I was writing about it was my pain. It seemed to be a good way to show my confusion about what it was I was dealing with in this child, my feelings of isolation and my need for comfort.

So far so good, but I also knew that the reader was likely to ask why Paul (autism or no autism) would lie down in the middle of a busy London street in the first place. I needed to motivate his action, even if in reality it had come out of the blue and seemed to be completely unmotivated. So I began to invent. I created a scene outside a greengrocer's in which Paul pulled an apple out from under a pyramid of apples, causing them all to cascade onto the sidewalk. This made the child very unhappy, obviously. But I decided to set the stage further for the street episode which was to follow. So I created another little scene in which I tore around a grocery store grabbing the items I needed to cook that evening, all the while shoving a screaming Paul back into his seat in the grocery cart. This is what I wrote:

> Grimly whipping around the aisles (I *had* to finish this shopping), I stuffed food almost at random into the cart, running to find the few things Paul would eat and the supplies we needed for dinner

that night. Mint sauce, raisins, milk, rice, Cheddar cheese.

By now it was hard to ignore the panic in Paul's voice. Several times other shoppers, staring at me with stony faces, seemed about to say something, then quickly glanced away. Other children had stopped their crying and were staring with fascination at Paul.

Coming up at last to the checkout lines, I saw they were all full, I would have to stand here and wait with this screaming child. I kept shoving Paul back down into his seat. Then feeling terribly guilty, I would try to comfort him. But he was beyond comfort, way beyond it.

Then I caught sight of a display of lollipops, the candy that Jim sometimes used for bribing Paul. I had been very determined to try to keep this candy away from Paul and was even rather censorious with Jim and his mother when they gave him sweets. But now I snatched a lollipop, the biggest one of all, off the rack. Tearing the wrapper loose, I stuffed it into Paul's mouth.

He gagged slightly, and started to take it out of his mouth, to howl again. But he stopped, midhowl, and started sucking on the lollipop, pausing just enough to catch his breath in hiccups. His face was streaked with tears and dirt. He looked a most forlorn, lost little boy, and I noticed other shoppers still watching us in a covert and deeply disapproving way. (Pages 36–37)

I have to confess this part never happened. And yet something like it did happen over and over again, in different ways, at different times. For example, Paul *was* difficult in grocery stores (and other crowded places). My husband *did* appease him with sweets (although I never did—I tended to buy him puzzles or toys instead, another form of bribery). So it made sense to put all this together in one scene at one time, to use the apple scene, then the grocery store events, to lead up to the moment in the street and the old woman's words—and the pain I felt, which was very real.

Some writers might not approve of this form of invention and prefer to stick closely to actual events, rather than partly reimagined ones, to use single memories rather than merged ones. But I think that memories do have to be reexperienced when we write about them, and frequently they have to be rearranged. If you are uncomfortable about relying so heavily on the imagination, the next chapter will offer alternative ways of dealing with these problems in memoir writing.

EXERCISES

(1) Take an event you did not directly experience, but which you want to write about, and deliberately interpolate yourself into the scene. Imagine the place, the light, the weather, etc. even though you cannot

know exactly what any of this was like at the time the event took place. You might say "I imagine that she must have seen . . ." or "I can see him entering the room . . ."

(2) Involve your reader in the scene, using such phrases as "If you enter the room on a cold winter's day . . ." Sentences inviting the reader (as "you") into the scene can break down possible defenses which a reader might have since you are writing about something unknown.

(3) Use words like "probably" or "perhaps." You might say something like "Perhaps he opened the letter at the end of the day . . ." Or "She probably wasn't aware of the accident until much later . . ."

(4) In general, be openly hypothetical in making up your scene. Your reader will be more likely to stay with you if you honestly acknowledge your ignorance as well as your ways of reconceiving a scene. Admit the things you do not know and use your writer's "license" to reconstruct lost information. Remember that the power of the memoir lies precisely in this honesty of voice, this willing exposure of self in telling what you do not know and in dwelling on those things that preoccupy you.

∼ 4

USING PHOTOGRAPHS
AND OTHER
DOCUMENTARY EVIDENCE

THERE IS A STRANGE kind of "presence" in pictures. We can see and feel and hold them in our hands. They are a material reality, an incontrovertible testimony to the truth of an occasion. Until the modern age and the possibility of manipulating pictures through technology, pictures *were* the truth. Even now, old family pictures carry a particular weight in our minds. Susan Sontag claims that family photographs have become a "defense against anxiety" for those individuals who feel themselves robbed of a past. They reinstate "symbolically, the imperiled continuity and vanishing extendedness of family life." Most of us, in fact, have had the experience of opening a family album and being filled with a sense of the past which is suddenly *there*, a part of our present reality.

Photographs are a wonderful resource for the creative nonfiction writer. In this chapter you will find passages about photographs, as well as some suggestions of how to write about pictures. But there are other forms of documentation which will also be discussed here, such as medical records, deeds to land, job evaluations, and the like.

Even these examples will not exhaust all the possibilities. As you start to write, you might want to consider not just letters, diaries, journals, and photo albums (all commonly mentioned sources), but also the resources you can find in a library. If you are writing about a historical moment, you might want to look at period magazines and newspapers. Even the advertisements can trigger memories of a time you thought you had forgotten. Many libraries have special collections of photos, papers, and artifacts.

If more specialized resources are not readily available to you, a good local reference room of the library may supply useful material: encyclopedias and various kinds of dictionaries (of medicine, of navigation, plants, birds, etc.). *The Chronicle of the Twentieth Century* is a wonderful resource, as is *The People's Chronology*.

It never hurts to visit the place you are writing about. Visiting a childhood home or neighborhood as an adult lets you see the place in a totally different way—but it also is likely to trigger very sensual memories of experiences you have long forgotten. Many people say the sense of smell is possibly the most evocative of all the senses in recalling a place or a time. The slight smell of gas from a stove always takes me back to my grandmother's kitchen. Then I think of the small rocking chair with the red cushion beside the stove, as well as the basement just beneath the kitchen where one aunt tried to grow mushrooms.

Photographs as a Resource for the Writer

Photographs are extremely valuable for the writer trying to remember or to reinvoke a past which seems to be gone. I sometimes ask my students to bring a photograph to class and to write about it. It's interesting to see what emerges, because there is often some new revelation, even from an old and very familiar picture. Having to write about it can make a photograph seem like something we are seeing for the first time.

Sometimes I ask the students to exchange photographs and write about someone else's picture. When we do this, we have none of the surrounding context for the picture, none of the family stories or memories which situate it within a particular time or place or meaning. We are simply describing what is there, what we see printed on the paper. And this can be a very useful exercise of the imagination.

I have often used pictures to restart myself writing when I felt I had nothing more to say. Once while I was visiting my father I was trying to write part of the first chapter of my book *News from the Border*. Years before this I had put together a set of pictures for him to hang on the wall of his library. Within a single frame I had collected many small prints of his children and his grandchildren. Now, sitting in that room, staring at that collection of pictures, I was suddenly able to write something about one of them.

One particular photo drew me in ways I didn't at first understand. It seemed to have a power that went far beyond the meaning of that single occasion. Here is what I wrote:

We spent Paul's first summer in France and England, and should have been very happy. I have a picture taken at this time: June 1973, our garden on the edge of the little village of Contignac in the south of France. Paul, at ten months and just learning to stand, is holding onto one side of a metal lawn chair. My seventy-three-year-old father, who has come with us to baby-sit while Jim and I write our dissertations, stands on the other side of the chair. He is looking at Paul. He has just taken a pebble from the corner of Paul's cheek. The sun comes through the green leaves of the lime trees; it shines through the wispy blond curls at the baby's neck. Both faces have a look of open innocence.

Every morning at that time, my father took the baby down the hill to greet an old man. This old man belonged to the farming family, and he was put out by his daughter to sit all day by the side of the road or, if it was raining, in the mouth of the mushroom cave. My father spoke no French, the old French man, who was deaf and senile, spoke no English. But with the baby, together they communicated. For them it was enough.

Looking at that picture now, I want to pick up the baby, to re-enter that time. I want to blow kisses through his silky hair, to plant them on his small, hard skull. I didn't know then the fragility of that moment, over which already the dark wing was passing. I didn't know, and wouldn't know for another fifteen years, that the brain cells had clumped differently at the base of that little skull, that the cerebellum was too small, the cisterna magna too large. (Pages 2–3)

Only after I had written and rewritten this passage did I discover that I was at least three selves within it. First of all I was the experiencing self who took the picture (how else would I know that my father had just removed a pebble from Paul's mouth). Even so, I wasn't a participant in that moment shared by grandfather and grandson; I was simply standing there, camera in hand, observing.

Later as I reworked this first chapter again and again, I realized this was how I wanted to show myself in the whole first chapter: I wanted to emphasize the fact that I was a watcher, a bystander, a witness to something I hadn't yet begun to understand. Paul's autism wasn't yet diagnosed (although the reader knows this will be a book about autism) and I was at this time merely an observer of behaviors I couldn't yet interpret. Only later after rewriting this passage many times did I discover that it was the picture that helped me to position myself in relation to the story in this way—as observer—in the whole first chapter.

But there is a second self in this passage, one who is not present in the scene itself. This is the person sitting in my father's house many years later, looking at that picture. The second self here is the recollecting self, the one that feels such longing for a past that never really existed, who feels a desperate desire for a pure untroubled past where the baby is whole and complete and there are no worries. This is the self that wants to pick up that baby and to hold him secure against the knowledge I didn't yet have in 1973, but do have as I am looking at this moment caught in time.

In other words I wanted to return to that past and to relive the innocence which the picture visually suggests. These are feelings which I (and many other late twentieth-century writers) would usually edit out as illegitimate, as sentimental. But by writing about them as evoked by a picture, thus separating myself in part from those feelings, I could acknowledge them.

Finally, there is a third self in this passage, one separate from the observer and the recollecting self. The third self enters this scene as a writer reconstructing both the moment when the picture was taken and all the succeeding moments of looking at the picture and remembering. As a writer I know that a few months before the moment of *looking* at the picture Paul had an MRI, a Magnetic Resonance Image scan, which showed that he had the brain abnormalities typical of autism.

So perhaps more than anything else this passage is informed by the present circumstances during which I started to write the book. Paul was fifteen, he was deeply depressed, and I feared for his life. It was a time when I was held in suspense, when I didn't know if we would go forward or not, if *he* would go forward or not. And while writing about that picture I was deeply aware of all of those feelings. There is a plurality of selves in this passage—I am picture taker, anguished viewer of a picture already taken, and writer of the selves who do both of these things—that I later realized I could evoke only through writing about a picture.

Truth and Lies in Photographs

Pictures can do other things as well. Mary McCarthy's *Memories of a Catholic Girlhood* includes old family photographs which tell the truth against the testimony of her cruel relatives who mistreated her and her brothers after their parents' deaths. But one of the pictures, as she points out, tells a lie. The picture shows her and her three brothers, as children, with a pony. It's a happy picture. It shows four privileged children who are lucky enough to ride ponies in the summer. Here is how she writes about this photo:

> One of the family photographs that has recently come to light shows the four of us children, looking very happy, with a pony on which Preston and Sheridan are sitting. We are all dressed up, I am not wearing my glasses, and my straight hair is softly curled. The pony was a stage prop. He used to be led up and down our street by an itinerant photographer, soliciting trade. The photograph, of course, was sent out west to the Preston family, who were in no position to know that this was the only time we had ever been close to a pony. (Page 85)

What the picture doesn't show is that the children are undernourished (their clothing and the soft focus hide that), that Mary has been regularly beaten for "telling lies," and that the toys sent to them by the relatives out West are put away on high shelves. It doesn't show these children put to bed every night with their mouths sealed shut by sticky adhesive tape "to prevent mouth breathing," nor does it show the tape being removed every morning with ether.

Reading the book, we are privy to all those secrets which Mary's uncle and aunts try so desperately to hide. The lie of the happy pony picture is all the more damning within the context of a whole "narrative" built by the adults who tell lies to the children and to each other, and within the context of the truth for which Mary is sometimes punished. But the lies go even deeper than this. Because their parents have died, the truth of the children's early experience is contested, and they are in a sense stripped of both language and memory. The people most likely to confirm their early memories have died and their guardians "rewrite" their early years by telling the children that their memories are lies.

Thus it is easy to see how important photographs would be to a story which has been reformulated by guardians as a lie or a "false" memory. Within this context, pictures become desperately valued. McCarthy shows the pony picture as a lie, but she also shows some true pictures of happy moments when she was a young child at birthday parties and outings with her indulgent parents before their deaths.

Other Resources: Medical and Other Documents

Family movies and videos are a wonderful resource for those who have been able to make recordings. But there are many other resources you may turn to: letters (other people's as well as your own), medical records, and legal documentation, for example.

Susanna Kaysen's *Girl, Interrupted* is an account of the author's breakdown and hospitalization as a young woman. Kaysen gives a direct, unmediated, sensory-based account of what it *felt like* to be in McLean Psychiatric Hospital for almost two years, at the age of eighteen and nineteen. Surprisingly, what she tells us is very funny. But she also offers us her medical records, which are very different from the direct account of the experience itself.

Think of the problems involved in writing such a book: telling the story of your mental breakdown and hospitalization at the age of eighteen has got to be a difficult task. Large parts of your memory might be wiped out through either drugs or the confusion of the illness itself. Even if you have vivid memories, you may be tempted to doubt their veracity. You also have the task of describing an experience many of your readers have never had and might fear. You have to take your readers across a border many of them don't want to cross, or at least to translate your experience into terms they can understand.

Kaysen gives a brilliant, minimalist portrayal of the everyday life of the hospital: what patterns look like on the floor, the regulation "checks" on the patients every fifteen minutes, the feeling of time passing too fast or too slow. She does not give background, history, or information about her family. Instead we get the impression that her life might have begun the first day in the hospital.

To give a sense of this experience, she describes it as a "parallel universe":

People ask, How did you get in there? What they really want to know is if they are likely to end up in there as well. I can't answer the real question. All I can tell them is, It's easy.

And it is easy to slip into a parallel universe. There are so many of them: worlds of the insane, the criminal, the crippled, the dying, perhaps of the dead as well. These worlds exist alongside this world and resemble it, but are not in it. (Page 5)

So what place does medical documentation have in this portrayal? Interestingly, *Girl, Interrupted* includes Kaysen's photocopied hospital admission and discharge records, diagnostic sheets, and the standard description of "Borderline Personality Disorder" taken from *The Diagnostic and Statistical Manual of Mental Disorders.* These pages, however, seem to have little to do with the description of the experience itself. It's as if these two forms of writing exist in parallel universes.

I suspect that Kaysen was really stung by her medical records. At times they sound very damning, as in the following passage about Borderline Personality Disorder:

An essential feature of this disorder is a pervasive pattern of instability of self-image, interpersonal re-

lationships, and mood, beginning in early adult-
hood and present in a variety of contexts.

A marked and persistent identity disturbance is
almost invariably present. This is often pervasive,
and is manifested by uncertainty about several life
issues, such as self-image, sexual orientation, long-
term goals or career choice, types of friends or
lovers to have, and which values to adopt. The person often experiences this instability of self-image
as chronic feelings of emptiness and boredom.
(Page 147)

Obviously, Kaysen has to engage with this description at a certain point in the narrative, and she does
so at the end. "So these were the charges against me.
I didn't read them until twenty-five years later," she
begins the chapter called "My Diagnosis." Then she
comments: "It's a fairly accurate picture of me at
eighteen, minus a few quirks like reckless driving and
eating binges. It's accurate but it isn't profound."
(Page 150)

This kind of documentation is not used to confirm
the reality or authenticity of the experience, but
rather to drag against the reality of the experience
itself. It's the discontinuities between the medical understanding of her breakdown and the writer's direct
perception of it that is the point here. We see from
this example how documentation can be used ironically to raise doubts in the reader's mind, or to leave

certain issues unresolved, such as the question of who's "right" and who's "wrong" about the possibility of full recovery.

Of course Kaysen is the writer of the book, so in the end she has to be the one who is right. At least she has the last word. She is the one who chooses to position these documents in a certain relationship to the text itself. And since the documents appear in a disruptive way and are not really integrated into the text which tells the story of the experience itself, we tend to trust them less than we would have if she had given them a more authoritative position.

As you write about your own difficult experience, you might want to do the same thing Kaysen does: simply present documents as a parallel account of an experience you also convey directly, without resolving the differences between the two points of view. Divorce proceedings, medical files, school reports, or annual reviews given for your job might all be useful in this way. They can either verify the truth of a memory, or they can be used ironically, as Kaysen uses medical records, to show the gap between official records and felt experience.

Here is another example in which the writer, a friend of mine, uses the personal statement for her tenure evaluation (which she must write, but which she finds herself unable to write) as an ironic way of introducing us to her complex past. She meets with the Dean of the college:

Nothing ever changes. Here I am unable to do my work.

The college has never exempted anyone in the process of going through tenure from writing a self-evaluation, Raymond says. He looks surprised about my request.

He is sitting on the other side of the table with the new books published by his faculty, with the *Smithsonian*, the *New Yorker, A Brief History of Time* and *The Closing of the American Mind.* There is more, buried under another stack of papers. He leans back, his elbows on the arms of the chair on which the name of the college is printed, the tips of his finger touching as if in prayer. But he keeps his eyes open, a rare thing since intense reflection usually forces him to talk without the distraction of the visual sense, eyes directed towards the ceiling or maybe the sky above. And since the issues of the college require him to think with intensity and concentration, most of his meetings take place, for him, in the dark, and for his partner, in the uncertainty as to whether the dean knows with whom he is talking.

How about making an exception, I say. It can't go on like this. I have tried every week-end of the term, and every time it was a failure . . .

The dean and the tenure candidate go on talking about what is expected in this sort of evaluation. He continues to try to soothe her with a series of reassurances, but she cannot reconcile within herself the discrepancy between the public and private parts of her story. Instead, she begins to tell us, her readers, something about herself, her sense that she has somehow betrayed her family left behind in Germany. Then she says to the dean:

> You don't expect, I say—I mean, you wouldn't want to see my family trekking through the winter of 1945 and getting caught in the bombing of Dresden, and nearly freezing to death on the road, or say, the way they survived later—you wouldn't want to read that in a statement about my professional development for a tenure evaluation!

Aha, we—her readers—think. This is the core of a wonderful and terrible story, but who would have thought that a writer's block over a tenure statement could yield such rich material? Ironically, it is just the right device for beginning such a story. The naively optimistic conventions of a tenure statement ("something about offering to open the young minds of our students with the precious perspective of a foreign language . . .") provide the perfect foil for the deeper and more traumatic story.

Using Legal Documents

Legal documents—deeds to land, marriage, birth, and death certificates, divorce documents, adoption records, wills, records of court proceedings, and other such things—are also very useful in generating material for writing. The language in these different kinds of documents can be used to great effect, especially when we really don't know much else about the events they recount.

In a piece of unpublished writing, I used legal documents to try to discover something about my grandmother's home in the Shenandoah Valley. This is a place I grew up knowing through childhood visits, yet feel I cannot know in a deeper sense. The house and farm have preoccupied me all my life, partly because they have been in the family for more than two hundred years, yet they seem lost to me now. Here is what I wrote:

Recently my uncle sent me some xeroxed documents from the county historical society concerning the land and the family. One is a will dated July 22, 1806. Another a deed of property dating from the twentieth day of August, 1765. On that date "James Trotter and Mary his wife, of the county of Augusta and Colony of Virginia Plantation," sold the land to my family, for the sum of "90 pounds current money of Virginia."

This place is described as "one certain tract or parcel of land containing one hundred seventy acres lying and being in the County of Augusta." With the land, the family also received "all Houses Buildings Gardens Orchards Improvements Wood and Trees Marshes Swamps Meadows Ways Waters Water Courses Easements Profits Commodities hired tenants and appurtenances . . ." To this "William Sproul and his heirs" the document says, "will go all Privileges Incomes Advantages and Appurtenances."

To me the language of this document is wonderfully rich because it is so much of its time and place. But legal language, even today, is archaic and therefore well suited to providing a very different view of property, for example, than actually living on the land would provide. As I thought about this language, I began to realize both its aptness and its ironic distance from the house and farm I knew so well as a child. I tried to explore this difference:

One tall order, I think. But nothing less than the truth. It is not just this William Sproul who received all this, but his heirs who were and are named William Sproul. Or if not William Sproul, then at least John Sproul. In the house there is not a single picture of my mother, who was born there and lived there all her childhood, the eldest child of her generation, nor is there a picture of my grandmother who lived there for sixty-five years.

In fact, of course there is not a single picture of many of the people who lived and worked on this land. I learn that, before a member of the family suffered reverses in a distillery business and had to pay off a note that had been secured by several farms and other property, my great great grandfather and his cousins held thousands of acres in this valley. And there was only one way—that I know of—to amass this kind of property in early nineteenth century Virginia, and only one way to work it, to turn it into productive land.

The family story of this lost property and distillery brought me to another, darker story, one which few members of the family want to talk about today. Again it is a legal paper, in this case a will, which tells the story both so vividly—and so inadequately.

Another document tells this story. There they are—among handsaws, sausage cutters, 67 head of sheep, and one stack of inferior hay in the field; among bedsteads, looking glasses, Hymnals, Buck's Theological Dictionary, Blair's Sermons and Dick's Philosophy; among cotton bed sheets, guns and salt sellars; and exactly on the page between the bushels of corn "growing in the ground" on one side and on the other, "one measuring line and a pair of saddle bags"—seventeen slaves.

The inventory of the personal estate of John Sproul, deceased, "given under our hands this 26th day of September, 1849," includes seventeen slaves, each with their monetary value. Tom, at seventy, is valued at zero, Henry, who is twenty, is worth $550. Between them in value, are various children and adults. Hannah, a two year old girl, is worth $125. The boy Barclay, who is sixteen, but whose hip is out of joint, is worth only $25.

There they are. And this is their only record.

I felt, as I tried to begin writing about my family and their slaves, that the best way to approach the issue (so little mentioned today and sometimes in fact denied) was through legal documentation. The deed and the will don't lie. They are the truth—yet the way in which they tell the story is so very particular, so special to the times in which they were written, so different from the way we would tell that story today after so much history has been uncovered, and so many black writers such as Toni Morrison have written about the reality of slavery.

As I worked on that piece I wanted to exploit some of these differences in language. But I was also aware that, in a sense, this time of slavery was a past that is unapproachable—by me or by anyone else. Too much information is lost to us and slavery is too foreign to our present consciousness, even when that consciousness includes a knowledge of history, to write about it easily. Perhaps it is the very difficulties of approach which will in the end make the most interesting form of writing.

EXERCISES

In this chapter we have seen some of the ways in which documentation can be used to support and confirm memory, as well as ways it can be used ironically to suggest that the "experts," for all their pictures and medical records, might not tell the truth after all. To practice using such documentation, try the following exercises:

(1) Find a family photograph of an important occasion and write about it in the following ways:

(a) Write about the real "truth" of that occasion, perhaps telling a story which is different from the accepted meaning of the occasion or from your memory of that time.

(b) Write about the way the picture really tells a lie. For example, people who hate each other might be standing together and smiling for the camera, etc.

(c) Write from the different points of view of the participants within the picture. Give their differences from each other and from your own sense of that picture. You might want to interview the people involved for this exercise.

(d) Write about the picture from the point of

view of a later generation, perhaps one not yet born.

(e) If you are in the picture, write about it as participant, as later observer, and maybe even as writer exploring the past and speculating about what it might mean in the future.

(2) Look for documentation of your own personal experience written by others. This documentation might consist of letters written by a parent or spouse, a brother or a sister. It might be medical records, or legal records such as deeds or birth certificates. The language of these latter forms of documentation is often strikingly different from the language you use yourself, and the ironic distance between the two languages can inspire your writing and transform your story.

A STORY IN SEARCH
OF ITS SUBJECT
How to Find Your Plot

By now, you have learned something about trusting your memories (even if you still feel they are partial or flawed), you have discovered that the imagination can come to the aid of memory, and you have seen how you can use photographs or other forms of documentation to generate more material. Let's say you have gotten lots of *stuff* down on paper, but don't know where it is headed. You can't see the shape of the story yet. This chapter will help you discover your plot.

Notice I say "discover" your plot, not make it up or invent it. I say this because I believe plot is not something that is imposed on the story; it is something organic, arising from the material itself. In saying this, of course, I am making a distinction often made today between "plot" and "story." I am assuming that the story is a given, something found in life itself; the plot is the shape the story must eventually take—and it may not be obvious at first.

One of the first things I often ask my students to do at this stage of their writing is to outline the chapter of a book or a smaller piece which they have read. I've tried this myself when I have gotten stuck on thinking through my plot. It's an exercise I recommend because by looking at how someone else thinks through the issue of structure you will begin to see more clearly how you might organize your own piece. I suggest that you find a piece of writing which you particularly admire, and then take it apart bit by bit. Here are some elements to look for as you read, then again as you set out to plot your own piece of writing:

(1) Is there a question implied at the beginning? Or is there a central mystery which needs to be explored? By exploring their questions or mysteries, you can see how other writers have worked out a plot.

(2) Is there a "base" story behind your narrative or the one you are outlining? Another way to think about this is to identify the mythic substructure behind many pieces of writing. It may be the "American success story," the pioneer narrative, the Cinderella story, or the Prodigal Son story. It's surprising how often narratives build on a familiar base story which

readers will recognize and which will establish expectations to be fulfilled or frustrated in the new narrative.

(3) Where does the writer slow down and create a scene and where does he or she speed up and summarize? Try plotting your own piece by singling out the important moments where you might want to pause and develop a scene fully; then identify the material which might be summarized. This will determine how you will treat time in your narrative.

(4) Does the writer plot the piece chronologically, thematically, or, as frequently happens, both together? You might try developing themes in your own writing, as well as (or instead of) following a linear sequence of events.

(5) You might also consider how some pieces are plotted according to an emotional sequence, a sequence of feelings such as those often identified in the stages of grief. Some writers lay out their structure in this way, and it can work extremely well.

(6) Some writers develop their plot around the experience of reversal (of fortune or expectations) and revelation (the moment at which you begin to see what you could not understand before). This notion of plotting is as old as Aristotle, and it is particularly relevant to the crisis narratives of today.

I will examine in depth each of these six suggestions and the advantages of each method. You might find yourself using just one of these techniques for your own narrative, or you might discover that you really want to draw on most or all of them.

Asking the Questions

Stop now and think of those questions which generated your writing in the first place. Sometimes these are the deeper questions which you dare to articulate only after you have been writing for a while. As Marilyn Chandler claims in her book, *A Healing Art; Regeneration Through Autobiography*, "Questions define the zone of inquiry that gives a book its shape." (Page 111) Chandler finds that these questions are often posed quite explicitly and "In each case the writing is presented as a quest for answers to questions that break taboos, penetrate forbidden territories, name hidden things, and challenge basic beliefs." (Page 11)

An example of such a question is the one Paulette Alden, who wrote *Crossing the Moon*, a book on her journey through infertility, tells us that she asked herself. In answering the question "How did I come to be a woman without a child?" she must challenge some basic assumptions learned in her Southern upbringing which defined a woman who does not have children as "the most selfish woman in the world." She must also confront the conflict between her aching desire to have children and her equally strong wish to live the life of a writer unencumbered by children. The answers generated by this one simple question are found not only in the story of her medical treatments for infertility, but also in the story of herself as a writer and a "southern girl":

> So how was it, I wondered, that I had arrived at this point in my life: almost thirty-nine years old, no child? When I looked back, I could see why, and even when, I took a sharp turn away from motherhood. I could also see why motherhood would catch up with me. (Page 17)

This passage sets up the expectations we will have for the plot that follows. She lets us know that first she will explore that time of her life when she "took a sharp turn away from motherhood," and also that time when motherhood will "catch up" with her. Notice that she doesn't indicate here how she will resolve this seemingly unresolvable conflict. That enigma, as Roland Barthes calls it, will draw us forward through the narrative. We will want to know, above all, how she comes to terms with this conflict.

In her essay "Ruth's Song (Because She Could Not Sing It"), Gloria Steinem uses an equally compelling question in her short piece about her mother.

> Happy or unhappy, families are all mysterious. We have only to imagine how differently we would be

> described—and will be, after our deaths—by each
> of the family members who believe they know us.
> The only question is, Why are some mysteries more
> important than others? (Page 129)

The central question with which she introduces the
whole narrative is why her family never asked the
question about the causes of her mother's mental illness. The mystery is *why there was no mystery* in her
mother's progressively incapacitating illness, whereas
the changes in her Uncle Ed were a mystery worthy
of careful examination. To the others, her mother's
decline seemed merely to be a fact of life, since it was
sometimes the way of women to become "nervous"
and to succumb to paranoid delusions and hallucina-
tions.

> To the kind ones and those who liked her, this new
> Ruth was simply a sad event, perhaps a mental case,
> a family problem to be accepted and cared for until
> some natural process made her better. To the less
> kind or those who had resented her earlier inde-
> pendence, she was a willful failure, someone who
> lived in a filthy house, a woman who simply would
> not pull herself together.
>
> Unlike the case of my uncle Ed, exterior events
> were never suggested as reason enough for her
> problems. Giving up her own career was never cited
> as her personal parallel of the Depression. (Nor was
> there discussion of the Depression itself, though my

mother, like millions of others, had made potato
soup and cut up blankets to make my sister's winter
clothes.) Her fears of dependence and poverty were
no match for my uncle's possible political beliefs.
The real influence of newspaper editors who had
praised her reporting was not taken as seriously as
the possible influence of one radical professor [on
Steinem's Uncle Ed]. (Page 131)

You can see why such a question is startling and
how it could provide Steinem with both the entry
point of her narrative and its sequence of information. She understands why the fate of her Uncle Ed,
who changed from "brilliant young electrical engi-
neer to the town handyman . . . [living] in a house
near an abandoned airstrip" was "a mystery of importance in our family." But she cannot understand
why her mother's tragic transformation from compe-
tent young reporter, wife, and mother to a "terrorized
woman" who "was afraid to be alone, who could not
hang on to reality long enough to hold a job, and
who could rarely concentrate enough to read a
book," (page 131) is assumed to be a natural event.

This narrative has a larger social and historical
context (the Depression), but the specific question
was at first the smaller psychological one. Christa
Wolf, writing about growing up in Nazi Germany,
asks, "How did we become what we are?" but the ap-
plications of this larger political question are all per-

sonal in her book *A Model Childhood.* Elie Wiesel in *Night* asks about what happened to the Jews in Nazi Germany, but because his central questions are ultimately unanswerable, he answers in parables. Frequently he starts passages of his book with words like this: "Let me tell you a story."

Similarly, Susanna Kaysen begins her narrative about her mental illness and hospitalization when she was a young woman by asking the question she knew was on most people's minds: "How did I get in there?" which also implies the question "Could it happen to them?"

All of these writers are looking for answers to "questions that break taboos, penetrate forbidden territories, name hidden things, and challenge basic beliefs," as Marilyn Chandler notes. It is the question itself which generates the plot.

Finding Your "Base Story"

It is those stubborn questions that won't go away which can generate the most interesting narratives. In the case of Steinem's narrative, the uncle's life (thought to have been "corrupted" by one radical professor during the Depression) is taken as a kind of "base narrative," a story which produces the expected questions and the unsurprising answers. The uncle's story line is already plotted in a way; it is the story of the Depression. We have all heard it in one form or another. But the story of the housewife who had a "nervous breakdown" which "followed years of trying to take care of a baby, be the wife of a kind but financially irresponsible man with show-business dreams, and keep her much-loved job as reporter and newspaper editor," (page 131) is in a sense an unknown story.

In telling this story, Steinem follows the chronology of her mother's life history (reimagining her mother's feelings at various times), and at the same time follows her own growing awareness of her mother's life experience. At the end she sums it up in this way: "Dying seems less sad than having lived too little. But at least we're now asking questions about all the Ruths and all our family mysteries." (Page 146) It's not surprising that Steinem, as a major voice in the contemporary women's movement, ends her piece by encouraging all of us to begin to ask those unasked questions about our own mothers and grandmothers.

The base story of Eva Hoffman's book *Lost in Translation* is the immigrant story. But in this case, instead of extolling the virtues of coming to the new world from war-torn Europe, the story we are all familiar with as the immigrant-makes-good-and-lives-happily-ever-after, she writes against the grain. Hoffman tells her story as one of enormous loss. A language, a culture, a set of beliefs and expectations about how life should be lived—all are lost for her and her family. In her own case, she recovers, learns a new language and becomes acclimated to the new world. But for her parents the losses are permanent.

Natalie Kusz also writes with the immigrant story as the base narrative. In *Road Song*, the family (the father is already a refugee from Europe) moves from southern California to Alaska where they attempt to survive brutal winters as new immigrants. The story of Natalie's terrible childhood injury from a sled-dog attack is told against the background of the broader story of family survival in the wilderness. In this case, rather than question the base story, the writer tells it fully, as a story of heroic survival and the strength of a family that stays together in spite of almost overwhelming odds.

Scene and Summary: The Use of Time in Your Narrative

Earlier I pointed out the usefulness of identifying the important moments in your narrative, which may require you to slow down and write them out richly and completely. These are moments when you describe a place vividly, give dialogue, and dramatize an action fully. But there will be other instances when you will want to speed up and summarize months or even years. You certainly don't need to give every event in your life equal weight; if you tried to do this you would never finish writing.

As an example of skilled use of scene and summary, here is a passage from Tobias Wolff's book *This Boy's Life*, a story of child abuse and survival. The child, Tobias, has been sent ahead to live with his future stepfather, Dwight, while his mother finishes a job and packs up the old house. We already know that Dwight is stupid and mean-spirited, that he envies his young stepson and is out to get him in any way he can. The boy Tobias doesn't realize that he can tell his mother that he is miserable in this new home: "I was bound to accept as my home a place I did not feel at home in, and to take as my father a man who was offended by my existence and would never stop questioning my right to it."

Notice how Wolff moves from summary (in this case a summary of several months) into one particular vivid scene:

My mother finally gave Dwight a date in March. Once he knew she was coming he began to talk about his plans for renovating the house, but he drank at night and didn't get anything done. A couple of weeks before she quit her job he brought home a trunkful of paint . . . Dwight spread out his tarps and for several nights running we stayed up late painting the ceilings and walls. When we had finished those, Dwight looked around, saw that it was good, and kept going. He painted the coffee table white. He painted all the beds white, and the chests of drawers, and the dining-room table . . . it was stark, industrial strength, eye-frying white . . .

The narrative of the painting is interrupted here by an account of a phone call from the mother, followed by more summary, then it resumes with the immediate scene:

. . . Dwight and I finished painting the dining-room chairs. Then he lit a cigarette and looked around, his brush still in his hands. He gazed pensively at the piano. He said, "Sort of stands out, doesn't it?"

I looked at it with him. It was an old Baldwin upright, cased in black walnut . . . It was just a piece of furniture, so dark in all this whiteness that it seemed to be pulsing. You really couldn't look anywhere else.

I agreed that it stood out.

We went to work on it. Using fine bristles so our brush strokes wouldn't show, we painted the bench, the pedestal, the fluted columns . . . the carved scrollwork . . . the elaborate inlaid picture above the keyboard, a picture of a girl with braided yellow hair leaning out of her gabled window to listen to a red-bird on a branch . . . Finally, because the antique yellow of the ivory looked wrong to Dwight against the new white, we very carefully painted the keys, all except the black ones, of course. (Pages 104–106)

This is a fine scene and a wonderful place to stop and give more detailed information about the house the mother is soon to walk into. We know, of course, that life with this man will be disastrous. That one small scene of painting white everything in the house seems the perfect way to show how pathetic the man's efforts are, how controlled the child is, and how deceived the mother since she will soon enter a house (and a situation) that has been totally whitewashed.

Theme or Chronology?

Most narratives of personal experience follow some kind of rough chronology at least, but often writers rearrange the order of events for better effect. Furthermore, some information is usually suppressed, and certain events may be given more importance than they had seemed to have in "real life."

The modern literary memoir is frequently a very "shaped" book; it is a narrative which focuses on one particular event or crisis. Some people now draw a distinction between autobiography, which is a more or less chronological, responsible reporting of one's life history, and a memoir, which is a shaped narrative, written around a single theme. This is a distinction which I would like to uphold.

When I was writing my book about my autistic son, I struggled with what to include and what to leave out.

After all, if you enter a life anywhere, according to any subject, you will soon find that that subject connects with every other issue in your life. So how was I to decide what did and did not belong in a book about raising a child with autism? What other aspects of my life—my marriage, my other child, my job, my family of origin—belonged and would therefore enrich the narrative, make it seem full and more convincing? And which events or issues did not belong and would end up simply distracting the reader from following the story line? A consideration of plot always involves the question of selectivity, of what to include and what to omit.

In my own case, I tried to solve this issue by pulling back from the narrative and asking myself if what I was writing belonged here because in some way it had to do with the central theme of raising an autistic child. This was a story of our lives "under the aspect of autism." Many more things happened to each of us, and we can all (including my son) be summed up in many more ways than as people who have in some way struggled with autism, but that was the theme of this book.

Other recent memoirs do the same thing. Tobias Wolff tells his story under the aspect of abuse and escape from the entrapment of his life. Eva Hoffman tells her story under the aspect of her move from Poland to Canada at the age of thirteen, and the subsequent loss of her language and her culture. Lucy Grealy tells her life story under the aspect of cancer, Ewing's Sarcoma to be exact.

Lucy Grealy's book is worth considering in a little more detail. Her title tells us this is *The Autobiography of a Face*, and we know from this that her narrative will focus on questions of illness and recovery, on the surgeries and treatments she underwent, and of how all of this affected her sense of herself as well as her sense of her appearance.

But rather than present a simple chronology, Grealy begins at a midpoint in her narrative, when she is a teenager and has survived her surgeries and treatments and the cancer itself, but still has to come to terms with her appearance. Then she takes us back to the beginning, to the story of her being hit on the jaw when running around a grade-school playground. In later chapters, she brings her narrative to the end of this particular story of cancer survived, to the point where the title is no longer relevant. At the end of her book Grealy lets us know that the rest of her story will be an autobiography of much more than a face. So she ends her narrative there.

After her first chapter she basically tells her story roughly chronologically, but organizes each chapter around a theme. One of these themes is her love of animals as a child and this gives her the title and the organizing principle for many of the chapters, including one called "Petting Zoo." Interestingly, this zoo is actually a laboratory full of caged animals kept in the hospital for experimentation. When Lucy, together with some other children on her ward, persuade a candy striper to take them for a Sunday stroll through the hospital to see the "zoo," they discover a depth of misery far worse than their own suffering, bad as that is:

> Desperation saturated the room in those loud, whining cries, pacing back and forth, back and forth. I was overwhelmed. On each cage door was a sign with handwritten details about the dog, filled with alien words . . . Despite the warning, I let the dogs lick my fingers through the bars.
>
> The tenor of the expedition was shifting rapidly, taking on a slow, almost viscous quality. Our teenaged grownup tried to hurry us along, now aware that she'd made a mistake . . .
>
> It was too much now. There was a sound of monkeys in the next room, but we turned and left. In the elevator no one spoke; in the tunnels no one spoke. A sad, groping presence accompanied us all the way back to the ward . . . Sooner or later we all have to learn the words with which to name our own private losses, but then we just stood there in front of the nurses' desk, speechless. (Pages 51–52)

The scene of the children visiting the "petting zoo" is a way of conveying their own pain and confusion, and their need to find (eventually) the words

107

for their own losses. Many of Grealy's chapters work in this way. She chooses a theme through which she can both advance the story line chronologically, and explore a particular issue confronting the child as she faces her cancer treatments.

Plotting Through a Sequence of Feelings

A plot is, of course, more than the answer to a single question, and it is more than a reflection of a base story, a set of scenes and summaries, or an exploration of one particular theme. Plot implies a sequence of events, a beginning, a before and after, causality, etc. Memoir writing, fictive autobiography, the personal essay—all of these forms of personal writing have a plot, but the sequences found in those plots may be different from what you find in fiction. Frequently this kind of writing follows an emotional sequence; the plot outlines a progression in the feelings of the narrator or protagonist, rather than a sequence of events or actions.

In her book *On Death and Dying*, Elisabeth Kübler-Ross not only discusses the lessons we have to learn from the dying, but also gives us many small vignettes about specific people. Her work has been widely read and used to explain psychological processes we all undergo at various times in our lives, not just when we hear we are terminally ill. But I have also found her insights surprisingly applicable to writing, especially to plotting. Many kinds of stories which involve loss, change, or even radical questioning of the past, can be plotted according to the stages of grief she identifies: denial and isolation, anger, bargaining, depression, acceptance.

If you are writing about a significant loss or change in your life, you might consider the stages of grief. Even if the stages for you occur in a different sequence, you might plot your piece according to certain emotional stages using those events or vignettes which might demonstrate denial, for example, or bargaining.

Here, for example, are some details Kübler-Ross gives us about one woman who denied the bad news she had received about her health. This woman's very human response results in some intriguing maneuvers:

One of our patients described a long and expensive ritual, as she called it, to support her denial. She was convinced that the X-rays were "mixed up"; she asked for reassurance that her pathology report could not possibly be back so soon and that another patient's report must have been marked with her name. When none of this could be confirmed, she quickly asked to leave the hospital, looking for another physician in the vain hope "to get a better explanation for my troubles." (Page 34)

Details such as these are richly evocative and would make vivid first scenes of a piece of writing. Now imagine that you are writing about your own bad news—whatever it might be. How were you tempted to deny the news? Did you take specific actions to delay recognition?

To show how a single scene can be structured around an emotional state—in this case shock followed by denial—I will quote a passage from chapter 3 of my book *News from the Border*, where I am told by a doctor (the first specialist we consulted) that our son was retarded. Shock, isolation, then a strong reaction of denial, are expressed in this scene through some small visual details.

Dr. Tremain opened his office door and, staring at the floor, gestured with his hand for me to come in. Just inside the door, Paul pushed a chair against the wall, climbed onto it, and reached for the light switch. I took him down and tried to hold him in my lap.

"I believe your son is retarded" was what the doctor was saying. I stared at him, but his face was blurred and seemed far away, even though I knew he was right there, just across his desk on the other side of this bright, expensively furnished room. Dimly, I became aware that Paul was struggling in my arms. I was holding him too tightly and I loos-

ened my grip. Paul wiggled his shoulders and tried
to slide out of my grasp and onto the floor, but I
lifted him back onto my lap and stared at the doctor
over his head.

The sound of the doctor's voice seemed to be
coming to me in waves. I caught "probably only
moderately retarded," then heard "need to run
some tests."

Retarded. Suddenly, and intensely, I wanted Jim
there beside me. But then I knew I didn't want him
there. None of this would be true without Jim there
to hear it. I stared at a heavy crystal ashtray on the
table beside me. Paul picked up the ashtray and was
about to drop it on the glass-topped table. I caught
it just in time. (Pages 17–18)

Oddly, it was that crystal ashtray which I remembered
most vividly about the scene. It was only in writing the
scene later that I realized how symbolic (almost too
heavily symbolic) it was. I decided to use the detail
anyway, trusting my memory as a storehouse of important images, and believing that "we only store
memory images of value," as Patricia Hampl has reminded us.

But it was my shock, numbness, disbelief, and my
stangely irrational form of denial—none of this could
be true without Jim (my husband) there to hear it—
which I mostly wanted to get across to the reader at
this point.

Plotting a Whole Piece Around a Moment of Revelation

The scene above shows a moment of "reversal," the moment when bad news is given and the course of a life history changes. Another major moment in a narrative is the one in which something is realized or understood for the first time. In thinking about your own piece of writing, you might try to answer questions such as these: "When did I realize that I would not be able to go home . . . ? My mother was going to die . . . ? I had a serious illness . . . ? I would have to start over in my life . . . ?" By answering your own such questions, you may see where your story is headed. The meaning of the events may begin to unfold for you.

Here is an example from the writing of a young person—my daughter, a student in her last year of high school. This little college application essay might have grown from the sentence, "I first realized that. . . ." Here is what my daughter wrote:

I remember sitting in my Granddad's musty house on a rainy afternoon, and waiting for something to happen. I was probably only fourteen at the time, and I wanted desperately to go to the beach. But no, I had to sit and wait for the weather to clear before I could do anything. His house was a stone pillar, it seemed that nothing came of anything there, nothing ever happened. And my granddad was the same in a way, he was just a fact of life. He was immortal. He was in his nineties at the time, and he still had good health. The only things that were wrong with his health were that he was near-sighted, and he had lost a lot of hearing. He still had a thick mop of iron-gray hair. And he still lived in his own house in the middle of nowhere, a place he named Achahtee (which is Ithaca backwards, but with two "E's" instead of an "I" at the end). He still smoked his pipe on the back porch, and he still read a lot of books. In fact, he was the most well-read person I have ever known.

Then, this rainy afternoon, he came up to me, pointed to the drenched window, and asked me to tell him what rain sounded like. He couldn't remember, he said, it had been so long. I was shocked, I didn't know what to say. I couldn't answer him. I babbled something at him, the first thing I could come up with, and was left completely stricken as he walked away, and for a long time after. I knew that he was hard of hearing, but he had just showed me what it was like to be old and to lose something so simple and so precious as the sound of rain. He was no longer immortal to me.

This passage provides the needed framework for an essay reflecting on the death of a much-loved grandfather. However, the death itself isn't in the foreground of the piece. It is the grandfather's deafness and his inability to hear or even remember the sound of rain which teaches her the terrible truth: he is not a fact of life, he is mortal and will someday die.

His death follows almost naturally in the writing, after that one shocking moment of revelation several years before. This piece is a small crisis narrative, in which the writer comes to terms with the fact of death.

EXERCISES

(1) Start by outlining the plot of a chapter of a memoir, or a smaller piece of writing. Write out the order of events as given, the order of the information that is given, the moments when the writer pauses to give us a scene and when that writer speeds up to give a summary of events, etc. Now apply what you have learned to your own writing.

(2) Look at what you have written so far. Step back and see if you can sum your story up in one sentence: "This story is about . . ."

(3) Now that you have identified the central subject matter of the story, ask yourself "What is the mystery?" or "What is the central question?" What is the reader most likely to ask of this story? What did you not know when you started to write?

(4) Use the stages of grief identified by Elisabeth Kübler-Ross as a plotting device to explore an expe-

rience involving unwelcome change or loss. Try to find moments in your own narrative which might demonstrate each of the feelings she identified: denial, anger, bargaining, depression and acceptance. Then write a short scene around each one.

(5) Decide which parts of your narrative could be written as summary, condensing a large sweep of time into a paragraph or two. Then decide what events are so revealing or so striking that they must be written out as scenes. Slow down at those moments and write out the event as completely as you can.

(6) Look for your themes in the midst of a chronological telling. You might find that you want to reorganize passages (or chapters) around these themes.

(7) Look for the "base story" in your narrative. This might be an oft-repeated story such as the Cinderella story about the youngest and poorest and most abandoned child, whose life comes out right in the end. It might be a narrative like the old man Lear's story of betrayal and rage, followed by reconciliation. It could be an immigrant's story or a story of the frontier. You might discover that you are really writing a story of exile, or of a paradise lost. Look for the familiar story behind your own, then write either with it or against it. Use your own story to confirm or to question the wisdom of time-honored stories.

(8) Identify the moment at which you realized something important and write your story around that moment of enlightenment. This can be a "before and after" story, and you can use the moment of revelation at several different possible places in the narrative. You might start the narrative with it, then move backwards in time to the "beginning" and then forward again to the end. Or you might save that moment for the very end of your narrative. Experiment with different ways of doing this.

THE SELF IN THE STORY
Finding Your Voice

THE VOICE OF THE NARRATOR in a memoir should be
a trustworthy one. An unreliable narrator, interesting
as that might be in fiction, wouldn't work at all in
nonfiction. The writer of memoir enters into a particular kind of contract with the reader, declaring that
the narrative is a true one, and to convince the reader
to keep reading the voice must be trustworthy. The
reader must never sense that some important information is being withheld, or that the narrator is being
manipulative or self-serving. Even over-arguing or
over-explaining something can turn your reader off.
This chapter is designed to help you avoid these pitfalls and to develop a strong, likable "self in the
story."

Establishing a reliable narrator doesn't mean that
the writer cannot expand on or reimagine the truth.

As we have already seen, imaginative recreation of re-membered events is an essential part of the memoir. But the narrator must sound trustworthy even when exercising the imagination.

But what is this "voice" in the memoir? When we discuss reading and writing today, we often hear talk about voice, and it can mean a number of things. First of all, it suggests style, habits of speech, what we sound like in spoken or written language. Voice also means attitude, our approach to what we are writing, what makes us angry or sad or happy. In other words, voice is the personality behind the storytelling. And of course it is this voice, more than the story itself, which will finally determine whether or not the writ-ing is interesting to your reader.

I didn't raise this issue earlier because I have found that when we become too self-conscious about our voices, we can become intimidated and stop writ-ing. It is often more productive to write out a lot of your story before you step back and begin to consider matters of voice. About two-thirds of the way through a class of mine, I begin to talk to my students about this subject. One of the things I tell them is that after a short time of hearing them speak and hearing their voices in writing, I can usually tell whose paper it is I am reading, even if they leave off the name. There are rhythms of speech I begin to hear, habits of phras-ing, a certain sense of humor, maybe a particular use of irony. Some of the voices are straightforward, even bold. Others tend to be more intimate, almost innocent-sounding, yet revealing. Some are quiet, others more flamboyant. And all of them speak with these voices more or less unconsciously.

Nevertheless, there is still a lot that happens to a speaking voice when it turns into a writing voice. The challenge here is to maintain the individuality of the voice and at the same time appeal more generally to the reader. How do you create a voice that is trustworthy and interesting at the same time? How do you project a personality in your writing without getting in the way of the story itself?

In what follows, I will discuss matters of honesty and discrimination (what you choose to tell and what you want to leave out), then I want to distinguish different possible voices in your narrative. It is important to note that the narrator is frequently separate from the protagonist. Both are aspects of your writing and of who you are, but they might emerge as different voices in your narrative. Some of the exercises and examples which follow are designed to help you distinguish these different voices and use them appropriately.

Finally, I will explore another aspect of memoir writing which is very important, and that is the musing or reflecting voice. This voice neither presents a dramatic scene, nor summarizes events, but rather pulls back from the narrative and thinks out loud. It is this musing voice which can be most distinctive in the memoir; in fact, it may be the most compelling feature about memoir writing at this moment in time.

Honesty

Honesty is vital when writing a first person narrative. A memoir is not the place for deliberate deception, evasion, or cunning. When we begin to write, however, we often feel the urge to tell all. We confuse honesty with confession, integrity with self-exposure. Some reviewers and commentators have fallen into the trap of comparing the new literary memoir with talk shows, where guests confess their darkest secrets without considering how this will affect other people or whether it is wise in terms of the rest of their own lives. Good memoir writing does not do that.

Remember, you can chose to tell or not. There may be some parts of your life history that you do not want to share with anyone, and you are under no compulsion to tell all. It is important that you take ownership of your story and understand that you can choose how to tell it.

Learn to "listen to the story." The story will tell you what needs to be included. This can be a hard concept to grasp, since you are always aware that the story you are telling has already happened, and thus is already fixed in a certain form. Nevertheless, a memoir writer, like a fiction writer, must learn to step back and listen to what the story is trying to tell them.

The same principles that guide good fiction also guide us in writing effective nonfiction. In fiction writing we are encouraged to think of what belongs in the story, not what happened in life, and that's exactly what you should do in nonfiction writing too. The same principles of selection (what to include, what to omit) belong here as well.

Admitting Your Flaws

An attractive voice in personal narrative is one with flaws. None of us wants to read about a perfect person who has every problem under control and who never suffers any doubt, uncertainty, or fears for the future. Even in a memoir, we must not be too wise too soon; we can't be wise before wisdom is earned through experience and through making mistakes. We can't be a six-year-old knowing what we know at forty, nor can we remove ourselves so far from a scene of suffering or uncertainty that nothing is left for the reader to feel or discover.

At some point while I was writing *News from the Border*, I began to realize that, if I wanted to tell the story of my son's autism, I had to admit more of my own flaws. Many of the books similar to mine left out this part of the story. Parents often seemed to be too heroic, too focused on the child, or just too shadowy. Even though ours was a success story, it was certainly not a miracle story, nor did I have all the answers, by

121

any means. I had to tell the dark side, and my voice had to be real.

This was very scary, because I quickly found out that I had to tell the story of my drinking and of my discovery that I had gone over the edge into alcoholism. I felt very exposed as I set out to tell this story. All those old fears of sounding like confessional television came back to haunt me. Furthermore, I began to think that if I wrote about what was really going on in my family, I would have to skip town when the book came out. Then I started having fantasies that I would sneak into all the book stores in the country and rip out pages 175 through 182.

More seriously, and from a purely writing perspective, I kept wondering if a story of alcoholism really belonged in a story about autism. I didn't want this story to take over, to swamp the central theme. I needed to admit my mistakes, but not dwell on them for so long as to distract the reader from the story of me as the mother of an autistic son. Here is what I finally wrote:

I sat at the kitchen table, a glass of sherry at my elbow. A copy of Edith Wharton's *The House of Mirth* lay open before me; I had one hundred pages left to reread before class the next day, but I didn't feel ready to face Lily Bart's agonizing death through an overdose of chloral hydrate. I was fed up with her this time around. Spread open on top of the book was a *Family Day* magazine that I had picked up earlier that afternoon at the grocery store checkout stand. A stew bubbled on the stove, Paul was playing with his pipes and the hose in the backyard, Kate was still next door at the day-care center. I would have to pick her up in half an hour, but for now I was just sitting there, idly flipping through the magazine, sipping sherry.

I circled one page in the magazine, glancing at it, moving on, then flipping back: "Do You Have a Problem with Alcohol?" was printed in bold, blurry letters at the top of the page. Then underneath, the author suggested that I "take the easy ten-minute test."

Taking a large sip from the glass of sherry, I picked up a pencil and started marking the answers:

1. Have you ever felt guilty about your drinking? (Well, yes. Hasn't everyone?)

2. Do you drink to feel better about yourself? To handle stress? To feel normal? To reward yourself after a hard day's work? (Yes to all of these. What's a drink for, anyway?)

3. Have you ever had a blackout when you were drinking? (No, what *is* a blackout? Sounds awful.)

4. Has your family suffered financially because of your drinking? (No! Of course not.)

5. Have you ever been in trouble with the law because of your drinking? (Heavens, no.)

6. Have you ever missed work because of your drinking? (Of course not. But, I wondered, what

about all those sore throats and cases of flu I am always getting?)

Well, what about them? I paused to look out the window. Paul was soaked, but I decided he was good for at least another ten minutes. He had built a dam on the sidewalk with rocks and sand, and he was absorbed with flooding it with the hose, trying to see how much pressure the dam would take before it gave. Sand and rocks were all over the edge of the lawn, as well as the sidewalk. I knew Jim would be furious when he came home, but what could I do, how could I take care of everything anyway? I poured myself another large glass of sherry and went back to the questionnaire. (Pages 175–176)

As you can see from this passage, I tried to find a way of telling this story humorously (it gets more serious later in the chapter), but also to bring the matter of my own flaw—my drinking—back to the main story of autism as seen in the passage about the child flooding the yard. I also used the scene as a way of showing the dissention between my husband Jim and myself. The significance of my drinking emerges, but does not overwhelm the central story about raising a son with autism.

The Humorous Voice

What I am about to discuss next is pretty obvious; nevertheless, it needs to be said. There is humor in almost any situation (as you can see from the example above), and sometimes a tragedy can look ridiculous if viewed from another angle. Furthermore, when we trust ourselves (and our voices) enough to be willing to see how funny some events were, we immediately solve one of the problems of memoir writing, and that is the temptation to be too solemn.

As we saw earlier, among the pitfalls we fear when we begin to write the story of our lives is the fear that we might sound too "special," that we might act like a tragedy king or queen, as though no one has ever suffered as we have. This might be acceptable if we are writing about other people, but when we take ourselves too seriously, we can sound insufferable.

The scene above depends on humor to express this painful revelation. But sometimes a whole book is funny, relying on comedic devices to carry us through a story of great suffering. Two recently published books do this: Mary Karr's *The Liar's Club* uses the American tall tale and Frank McCourt's *Angela's Ashes* uses Irish stage routines. Both are stories of terrible childhoods, of poverty, neglect, and the ravages of alcoholism or mental illness in a parent. They are also survivor's stories that use humor to tell us the writers have survived intact enough to laugh at their pasts.

In the following passage from McCourt's book, the family is living in Limerick, in a small house next to a lavatory installed in Victorian times to serve the whole neighborhood. Frank and his brother Malachy come home from school one day to discover that the neighborhood toilet has overflowed into their kitchen.

Two weeks before Christmas Malachy and I come home in a heavy rain and when we push in the door we find the kitchen empty . . . There's a noise upstairs and when we go up we find Dad and Mam and the missing furniture . . . Mam tells us there was a terrible flood, that the rain came down the lane and poured in under the door . . . People emptying their buckets made it worse and there was a sickening stink in the kitchen. She thinks we should stay upstairs as long as there is rain. We'll be warm through the winter months and then we can go downstairs in the springtime if there is any sign of a dryness in the walls or the floor. Dad says it's like going away on our holidays to a warm foreign place like Italy. Malachy says the [picture of the] Pope is still on the wall downstairs and he's going to be all cold and couldn't we bring him up? but Mam says No, he's going to stay where he is because I don't want him on the wall glaring at me in the bed. Isn't it enough that we dragged him all the way from

126

Brooklyn to Belfast to Dublin to Limerick? All I want is a little peace, ease and comfort. (Page 96)

One of the pleasures of this scene is the attractiveness of the voice. The child tells the story in all innocence, reporting simple fact and relating straight what other members of the family said. The words of these other characters are woven into the texture of the narration: "Malachy says the Pope is still on the wall downstairs and he's going to be all cold and couldn't we bring him up? but Mam says, No, he's going to stay where he is. . . ."

This kind of narration isn't easy to achieve, and it can even get a bit tiresome if you overdo it. But you might try using this kind of voice if the speech you grew up with is an unusual dialect, or a highly flavored local form of speech. Here is another passage from McCourt's book which exploits some ethnic differences in language and custom. The mother is trying to get some meat for their Christmas dinner, but all she has to pay for it is a "docket," which is rather like food stamps:

No goose, says the butcher, no ham. No fancy items when you bring the docket from the St. Vincent de Paul. What you can have now, missus, is black pudding and tripe or a sheep's head or a nice pig's head. No harm in a pig's head, missus, plenty of meat and children love it, slice that cheek, slather

127

it with mustard and you're in heaven, though I suppose they wouldn't have the likes of that in America
where they're mad for the steak and all classes of
poultry, flying, walking or swimming itself . . .

Mam says the pig's head isn't right for Christmas and he says 'tis more than the Holy Family had
in that cold stable in Bethlehem long ago. You
wouldn't find them complaining if someone offered
them a nice fat pig's head.

No, they wouldn't complain, says Mam, but
they'd never eat the pig's head. They were Jewish.

And what does that have to do with it? A pig's
head is a pig's head.

And a Jew is a Jew and 'tis against their religion
and I don't blame them.

The butcher says, Are you a bit of an expert, missus, on the Jews and the pig?

I am not, says Mam, but there was a Jewish
woman, Mrs. Leibowitz, in New York, and I don't
know what we would have done without her.
(Page 97)

The reality behind this little butcher-shop vignette
is three malnourished children waiting at home for
something to eat, three others dead from starvation
and disease, a husband who drinks up the week's
wages if he is lucky enough to get a job, and no coals
for cooking the pig's head if she does take it.

As you can see from these two passages, the
"voice" could very well be a stage voice; in fact Frank

McCourt appeared on the stage with his brother Malachy, doing an Irish musical revue about their childhood and youth. Written language is identical to spoken language here.

Here is another example of an informal voice which uses humor to deal with a sometimes painful subject. This is a passage from a "coming-out story" written by a student of mine. For a long time, when she was in high school, she couldn't admit to her friends that she wasn't really interested in boys. To get along with these friends, she made up crushes on boys which she didn't really have. Here she is with them, sitting in a circle, passing bowls of popcorn and Doritos and playing Truth or Dare:

> I tried explaining that I didn't like anyone. But in all actuality, I didn't really understand this whole *like* concept. I mean, it wasn't as though some guy made my palms sweat and my heart beat faster just by being near him. Guys were just, well, guys. No more, no less.
>
> "Everyone likes *someone*," they insisted again.
>
> Well, if *everyone* likes someone and since I'm included in that everyone category, I suppose that means that I do like *someone*. Besides even if I really don't I can't let them know that because then I would seem weird. And in eighth grade if you're weird, you're dead.
>
> "I guess I like Alan," I told them to satisfy my Truth or Dare requirement. And I supposed I could

like Alan. After all, he sat next to me in Social Studies and he laughed at all my jokes, so there could be some "like" there.

Unfortunately Alan liked me. And despite the rigid code of the pinkie swear, word got around that I liked him back. After the requisite awkward phone conversations, note passing and uncomfortable moments in the hall, Alan and I eventually titled ourselves boyfriend and girlfriend. We followed the eighth grade courtship rules; his parents drove us to and from the local discount movie theater where we saw *My Girl* and we attended the Valentine's Day dance together. Our relationship lasted the five months until school let out and then we drifted back to our status of being really good friends.

That was five years and seven fabricated crushes ago . . .

This student was writing some years later from a position of security, so she was able to look back on her younger self with that wonderful mixture of ruefulness and affection. She had learned how to separate the protagonist self (the eighth-grade girl fearful of losing friendships) and the mature narrative self telling the story.

The Voice of the Narrator and the Voice of the Protagonist

In memoir writing, unlike fiction, the voice is already chosen. The voice is yours—right? True, but that voice need not speak in a monotone; the voice of the memoir can be complex and various. For one thing, you may distinguish between yourself as the teller and yourself as the actor in the tale. Both the protagonist and the narrator are you, but often those two selves will come out sounding different.

The most obvious kind of narrative where this happens is that of childhood experience. A four-year-old child (you as protagonist of the story) will not have the same words or concepts which you have at your command later as an adult telling the story. You may want to write some passages in the child's voice, using the child's perception; in other passages you may reflect as an adult on that earlier moment in time.

Here is an example of how I wrote about an experience I had as a four-year-old child. The images are taken from the child's experience, but the perspective is that of the adult:

> Out of nowhere a memory came to me. It was . . .
> February 18, 1943, and I was on our front porch
> steps in Richmond, Virginia. My fourth birthday and
> I was sitting alone. Slowly, I kicked my heels back

against the brick steps. I think I was wearing leggings, but even through the wool, I felt the solid, hard dependableness of the world, where it began just at the back of my legs.

The pale southern February sun warmed my hands. The trees were lacy against the sky, the city hummed in the distance, and my mother was just inside baking a cake for my birthday. Very early that morning, before I was supposed to be awake, I had hidden behind a curtain to watch her wheel a small black doll-baby buggy, a second-hand carriage she had bought from a neighbor, up the walk and into the house. It was going to be my birthday present and I wasn't supposed to know it, but I was filled with joy, with the secret pleasure of a gift securely anticipated.

I was four years old and I felt an enormous satisfaction in that fact. My brother was just one, and I was pleased that he didn't even know it. And then, as if a kaleidoscope had shifted and a pattern suddenly came into view, I felt something I had never felt before. It seemed at that moment that I knew myself, knew who I was. I seemed to come into myself. I knew that I existed in the world. My heart was beating, the world glowed around me, and I was a part of it, a part of the living air, sitting there on the steps in the shimmering winter sunshine. And that knowledge alone was enough to fill me with an almost unbearable happiness.

I stopped kicking my heels against the brick and held myself very still, held myself for a small mo-

ment at the heart of the living universe. And knew
I had been blessed. (Pages 264–265)

In this passage, it is clearly the four-year-old child
who is proud of being four and feels superior to her
baby brother; it is she who hides behind the curtain
to watch her mother wheel the baby buggy up the
walk, who feels the sunshine on her hands and
the hardness of the brick behind her legs. But it is
the adult who narrates the scene, composing it from
memories. I know that, as a four-year-old, I did feel a
moment of enormous joy, but I could never have described it then in the language that I use now.

Sometimes it is helpful to work deliberately to separate these two voices, protagonist and narrator, in
your narrative. By doing so you can learn how to be
faithful to the experience of your former self, to give
all your feelings and perceptions and flaws of the
moment. At the same time if you want to direct the
narrative thematically, you can do so as a narrator
looking over the shoulder of your experiencing self.

An exercise I sometimes give my class is designed
to help you do that. Imagine a former self, yourself
at one particular time of your life, and describe that
former self, as if he or she were sitting across the
room. Describe clothing, gestures, the setting, etc.

After you have done this, stop and listen to this
former self. What is he or she trying to tell you? This
is part of the process of learning to listen to the story.

By doing this little exercise, you might begin to see ways in which you may have been putting words into the mouth of a younger self, and not really attending to the differences between your writer self now, and the self that was experiencing events in the past. Here is how one student used this exercise.

This is not me.

There she sits on the couch, curled up underneath a blanket. Her thin body is awkwardly spread out over pillows, feet hitting the end of the short couch . . . She is encased in an afghan blanket, enclosed by greens, reds, oranges. She looks like a worm, but she doesn't care. This is where she is comfortable.

Usually this is where she sits to do homework, positioned so that her knees support her reading. She studies her high school textbooks until her head begins to droop, and she nods off to sleep. Someone always enters the room in the middle of this, usually her father, and he tells her that she is not really studying or sleeping. She wakes up with a start then, saying that she is not really tired, that of course she can concentrate on her work now. Asks him to just leave her alone . . .

She sits on the couch weekday afternoons, studying-sleeping. Sometimes she goes there after dinner too. She is even there on weekend nights, when all of the other kids in school are out drinking, going out to eat, or watching videos at someone's house. She knows this because they always tell the stories before classes start again on Monday mornings. She hears the stories, knows that these are lifelong memories in formation. But, each time that the weekend comes, she just sits on the couch, curled up in a blanket.

Writing this was a kind of breakthrough for my student. She had started by writing about herself as a very good child and teenager. But as she got into the story more and more, she began to focus on significant losses in her life, including the loss of her grandmother who had died at her home. These losses were also somehow tied to the fact that she was such a "good girl," who asked so little for herself.

It was only when she began to see the "girl on the couch" and to listen to her that this writer began to see some of the connections between the different strands of her narrative. She now had an image for herself as withdrawn from all the activity that took place in the family. At the end of the narrative, however, after exploring her feelings of loss, she felt that she could become one with that girl on the sofa, and after that the girl was no longer trapped there. The writing enacted the escape, but only after the writer had first separated the protagonist self from the narrating self. Later my student merged the two selves in the narrative and no longer wrote of herself as "she."

The Reflecting Voice

One of the reasons that the literary memoir is making such a comeback, I believe, is that readers have begun to miss that more expansive voice, the musing, reflective voice that is willing to share an experience in all its fullness. It's true some novels still use that voice within a character or as part of an omniscient narration, but in recent years we have seen a great deal of clipped, minimalist writing.

The reflective voice is so important to memoir writing because self-revelation without reflection or understanding is merely self-exposure. We want the author of a memoir to have *grown up,* to have learned from earlier mistakes or experiences, and to be wiser for it. A writer who merely tells us (or even shows us) how awful life was will quickly lose our interest.

I have read a few books which are like this; they show the sheer awfulness of a life on drugs, or the unrelenting grief suffered after a spouse's death, but that is all they show. I usually stop reading these books before the end. If the narrator continues to wallow in "unprocessed" grief, on and on and on, I get bored—or worse, I get very irritated. It's not that I want all literature to be "uplifting," or every story to have a happy ending, but if there is no poetry and no understanding or insight, then I am left dissatisfied.

The reflecting or musing voice can also be a retrospective voice; it is the stance we take when we look back over events which have occurred in the past. And this voice is different from the one which does either scene or summary (which I talked about in the plot chapter), although sometimes one voice can move into another. The following passage from *This Boy's Life*, by Tobias Wolff, illustrates this.

When we are green, still half-created, we believe that our dreams are rights, that the world is disposed to act in our best interests, and that falling and dying are for quitters. We live on the innocent and monstrous assurance that we alone, of all the people ever born, have a special arrangement whereby we will be allowed to stay green forever.

That assurance burns very bright at certain moments. It was burning bright for me when Chuck and I left Seattle and started the long drive home. I had just dumped a load of stolen goods. My wallet was thick with bills which I would lose at cards one night, but which I then believed would keep me going for months. In a couple of weeks I was leaving for California . . .

Chuck felt good too . . . We sang along with the radio and shared a bottle of Canadian Club . . . The deejay was playing songs from two or three years before, songs that already made us nostalgic. The farther we got from Seattle the louder we sang. (Pages 286–287)

Notice how the voice here starts out as the reflecting voice ("When we are green, still half-created . . .),
goes on to summarize without refection ("I had just
dumped a load of stolen goods . . ."), and then enters
the scene itself ("We sang along with the radio and
shared a bottle of Canadian Club . . .").

A student of mine, a Latino who had been raised
by his Irish mother and her parents in a small town
in Oregon, was very interested in this scene and
wanted to figure out what made it work so well. He
wanted to find some way to explore the cultural dislocations he sometimes felt as a child of Mexican and
Irish American parents, and thought that Wolff's ex-
plorations of a different sort of cultural dislocation
would help him. This student went on to complete a
fine memoir piece, which included the following passage. It takes place after the death of his Irish grandfather, and he has been taken out of the house by
some of his uncles. The excerpt shows a rite of passage that takes place for him that day:

Johnny, Al, Joe and Tony are smoking Camel Reds
and pushing drinks around on the table. If there
were more glasses of beer it would seem like an odd
game of chess where no piece is bigger than another. They are silent at moments and laughing at
others. These are the four men I see most often
in my life, although Johnny less than others. . . .
They've chosen to come to the Riverside Inn tonight

after the funeral. The air in the house was suffocating—thick with grandfather's death. They wandered out of the house to this restaurant on the side of the river where "there would be music," someone had said. But we're sitting outside in weather that is almost chilly, and the door to the lounge is closed. We can only *see* the man inside, mouthing lyrics to a song.

I have gone through some odd rite of passage tonight.

—You hangin' in there kiddo?—asks Tony. I nod yes and Uncle Joe puts down a glass of something, rests his hand on my shoulder and smiles.

—Dominc's okay—he says to the rest of the group. Assuring them in some way that I wouldn't bust out and cry.—He's a strong kid.

～ ～ ～

Looking away from the patio and across the river I'm studying the weakness of the moonlight. It barely reflects the swirls and sway of the water. "This is the kind of night grandfather would hunt worms," I mumble to myself. I'm surprised though. I've caught myself in the act—because now I know that grandfather won't be out tonight. I've said it and I sit silently watching the other men around the table coming to this realization too.

This student moves from scene to summary to reflection at the end of the piece very skillfully. He doesn't completely pull out of the scene, as Wolff does by giving us a piece of wisdom about ourselves when we are young, but he does reflect on the meaning of what he has just said about his grandfather digging worms. This student went on to write about his growing awareness of the prejudice in his town towards Mexican Americans, and this scene after his Irish grandfather's funeral functions as a pivotal point where he moves from child to young adult.

The following exercises will help you to identify different possible voices in your own writing and to use them for writing reflection, scene, and summary, as well as for separating your protagonist self from your narrating self.

EXERCISES

(1) If at any point you get stuck in your writing, try to imagine your protagonist self as different from your narrator self. Sit that self across the room from you, and imagine him or her as different from your present-day self. Now take five or ten minutes to write a purely descriptive passage about that former self. Imagine clothes, gestures, attitude, body language, and so forth, but always keep to description, not evaluation or commentary.

(2) Now, try to listen to that earlier self. What does she or he have to tell you about that moment in time long ago? What does that earlier self know? What

does that protagonist self not know? Pick up your pen or pencil again and try to write down the words that earlier self is telling you about the direct experience of that moment in time.

(3) Look at books or essays you particularly admire and study the way in which the author uses different voices: the reflective voice, the voice which gives a summary, and the voice that enters into a scene completely.

(4) Write a humorous summary of a time in your past in which you admit your faults.

(5) Pick a moment in your past where you were young. Write about the moment using only the language you would have used at that time of your life.

(6) Now write about that same moment using the language you use today. Notice the differences in the two voices.

(7) Write about an event using the language of the participants in it, but not your own language. Use the habits of speech, the dialogue of the other characters, to give a summary of the scene.

~ 7

TO TELL OR NOT TO TELL

Ethical Considerations in
Writing a Memoir

EVERYONE WHO WISHES TO PUBLISH a personal narrative, and most people who write about their experiences struggle with certain ethical issues which have
to do with the lives of other people. If you are writing
family stories, and especially if you reveal family secrets, you may fear hurting people who are dear to
you. Or you may even be afraid of reprisal. If you are
writing about people who have done you some wrong,
you may fear other repercussions, maybe even a lawsuit. Think of the doctor that gave you a wrong diagnosis, the teacher who shamed you in front of the
whole fourth grade class, the uncle who hired your
father in his firm, then refused to pay him a decent
wage. Of course, you have grudges against all of these
people (or did at one time), yet you probably want to
resist sounding aggrieved or mean-spirited.

142

Even the most innocent description can sometimes displease. One of the things I have often thought about is that the moment we start to write we start to mythologize. We shape other people's lives into a form they may not approve of, or even recognize. We might choose their eccentricities as the most vivid way of giving a character sketch, and we think we are being affectionate. The person so portrayed, however, might very well not sense the affection, but instead feel embarrassed.

This might be a good time to return to the dialogue exercise from the beginning of the book, focusing specifically on your fears of exposure, embarrassment, or shame, as well as your fears of giving offense or of causing reprisal. Write a dialogue with those voices in your head that say you shouldn't be writing and you *certainly* shouldn't be thinking of publishing. Write out all your fears and consider them carefully. Some might be so strong and rational that you decide not to write certain passages, or at least not to show them to other people. In other cases, you might decide that your fears are largely groundless.

After you have identified some of your fears as groundless and others as too important to ignore, attempt to make some distinctions between those that remain. Use your common sense and decide where you want to rewrite, where you want to seek permission for publishing from the people involved, and where you feel you can go ahead and write exactly as you wish.

Libel and Invasion of Privacy

The most important of your worries, of course, is the possibility of a lawsuit claiming libel. Let's suppose that you are seeking to publish a piece in which you portray a real person in a bad light: the doctor who gave you a wrong diagnosis when she might have known better, the neighbor who harassed you by refusing to turn down the noise during loud parties or who put broken glass in your driveway.

Let's suppose now that you want to publish an account of these wrongs. In these cases, your editor and your publisher have an interest in seeing that your writing doesn't provoke a lawsuit. Once they have accepted a piece, they frequently ask their in-house counsel for guidance before publication, and you will need to follow their recommendations.

But what kinds of changes are you likely to have to make in your piece of writing before it gets published? When I published my first book, I was advised to change the names and identifying characteristics of the people who did some wrong to my son. Doctors, teachers, and others who made mistakes—and actually in almost all cases I would call what they did merely a mistake, since no maliciousness was ever intended—were disguised in this way.

144

With the doctors and teachers who had been obtuse, I just went ahead and wrote out the scenes in question. I took a lot of trouble to disguise their identities, however, giving them different names and different physical characteristics, and sometimes even combining several characters into one. I still had nagging feelings about one or two of them who were so kind and caring (even though they were mistaken about my son's diagnosis), that I hesitated to include them in the book. But I had to let the story itself tell me what belonged. I chose to tell of their mistakes, because they were an important part of the story of autism where misdiagnosis and even mistreatment is often a problem.

My son, in writing his afterword to the book, was much more concerned about telling the truth, the whole truth, and nothing but the truth. Perhaps because he has autism, he wanted strict accuracy in a way that I did not. I was much more concerned with getting the emotional truth of the story on paper, even if it meant changing chronology and the details of an occasion or a character.

In Paul's case, however, our publisher asked us to prepare statements to be signed by each of the people whose real names he had used. This is probably what you will have to do if you too wish to be strictly accurate. In these cases, the person has the oportunity to refuse to sign or possibly to ask for changes before publication.

145

In the case of public figures, the rules of the game are a little different. Usually, someone who is a public figure (an elected representative, for example) has a harder time bringing a successful suit against a writer and publisher simply because their lives are already more public. In such cases, however, you should write carefully and fairly. A mean-spirited or rancorous account might damage your own credibility as well as land you in legal trouble. Work hard on the tone of your writing, and when in doubt consult others, in particular your editor.

Family

Writing about family members can be a little trickier than writing about people whom you have known only in a casual or professional capacity. I struggled with my own hesitations and fears as I was writing my first book. At first I wrote only for myself and I wrote in pencil and in a notebook. Later, as the story began to grow and become an entity in itself, I began to "listen to the story." I was no longer so concerned with real people and real events, or with giving offense. The story itself began to carry me, to let me know what was important and belonged in an account of a family struggling with autism.

At that point I began to heighten some events that occured in my family and sometimes to combine several moments into a single occasion. I decided to allow the story to demand its own shape; and then I got out of its way. Many writers are very uncomfortable doing this. Like my son, they value strict verifiable accuracy more highly than I do. You have to make this decision for yourself. If you are writing about public or historical events, you should check and recheck your facts. If, on the other hand, you are writing a very personal story, as I was, your piece might turn out to be very close to fiction. In fact, some literature which is called "fiction" recounts events that are true in the strictest sense of the word.

Having said all this, however, I have to confess that my book did give offense to some members of my extended family. My immediate family was very involved in the writing of the book, in the sense that they read all passages where they appeared and they always had veto power over the way they were characterized in these passages. But others were, I felt, too far removed from the immediate story to have a stake in how it was written. I knew that if I stopped and consulted everyone who appeared in the book (or whose parents or sister or brother appeared in the book), it would never get written, much less published. So I decided to deal with the fallout later, and that is exactly what happened. Some people did say (usually indirectly through others) that they had been hurt by the way I wrote about my extended family. In one case, mentioning relative poverty was deemed shameful. In another case, portraying one part of my

147

family as worldly achievers (but not as scholarly) gave offense.

I brooded for months (and even years) over the ways I characterized my larger family, but never came up with a way of doing it differently. I felt that once I had made the decision to write and to publish I was bound to offend someone. Novelists I know have said the same. Even in a work of fiction, real people can find themselves portrayed in the story and take umbrage. Sometimes, in fact, they are even offended that they don't appear when others do.

Dealing With Family or Community Secrets

Writing about family secrets is one of the most difficult dilemmas you are likely to face. Just about all families have secrets they wish to keep hidden. Often there are different versions of what happened in the past. Sometimes over many years of telling stories, families re-create memories to suit some larger purpose, perhaps to protect an idealized version of themselves, even at the cost of "truth." Most of the time, they probably aren't even aware that they do this.

There are some important rules of thumb here, however. If you write about family secrets (the suicide of a great grandfather, the homosexuality of a cousin who is not "out," the feud between different family members that has gone on for generations, etc.), you might want to consult the people in question. If your portrayal of them is very revealing, show them passages and ask their permission to write about them in the ways you have chosen. In certain cases you should probably give them veto power.

In other instances, where the story is an old, old one and all the direct participants have long since died, you might decide just to go ahead and write. You may call or write to people who know the story or some part of it and give them a chance to supplement or even to correct your memory. Give them a chance to tell the story their own way and, if their interpretation of events is different from yours, get permission to include it. As we have seen in earlier chapters, this can add to the layers of narrative and enrich your writing immeasurably.

Some of my students wrote or called family members when they worked on pieces for my class. In most cases, a mother or a sister cooperated enthusiastically with the project, filling in bits the writer was too young to know or remembered differently. One student writer began passages of her narrative with direct quotations from her mother's letters. For another, a phone conversation with her sister concerning a terrible accident and injury suffered by the sister provided the perfect closure for her piece. This conversation moved both sisters to a new level of understanding, one which they might not have reached so quickly if the writing hadn't prompted the phone call. As they learned, life and art do sometimes intertwine in wonderful ways and writing can help us complete the process begun by living.

Sometimes, however, family secrets pose great difficulties for the writer. If you as writer insist on remembering accurately (as accurately as possible), you may be punished for holding on to the memory. Knowledge or memory can be experienced as a terrible burden. In fact, in every family, we are sometimes told, there is one member designated to hear the secrets of the past and then forbidden to retell those secrets. Maxine Hong Kingston's memoir of growing up Chinese-American, *The Woman Warrior*, which we looked at earlier, begins with the mother telling the daughter: "You must not tell anyone . . . what I am about to tell you. In China your father had a sister who killed herself. She jumped into the family well. We say that your father has brothers because it is as if she had never been born."

The mother burdens the child with a secret from the past which has been so repressed in official family history that the story about the dead aunt is a story about "No Name Woman." For the father, whose sister it was who gave birth to her illegitimate child in a pig sty then killed herself and her baby, "it is as if she had never been born." Of course, Kingston, like any bright child burdened with too much knowledge, must begin her wonderful narrative by telling this story. And thus a taboo is broken, a family rule violated, the aunt's story is told, and she is reborn in narrative.

A recent book, Seamus Deane's *Reading in the Dark*, also illustrates these different aspects of memory beautifully. The child in this narrative is never named (as Kingston never names herself in her narrative), his childhood is also lived among ghosts, and he too is burdened with an unbearable secret from the past. In this case, he grows up in Derry, in Northern Ireland, the second child of a Catholic family to which some terrible unknown betrayal has happened in the past. At first the "ghost" in the narrative is merely "a shadow," "somebody unhappy" sensed at the turning of the stairs by the mother who sends her young son downstairs until the ghost passes. The child expresses an innocent wish to stand beside his mother and face whatever it is she has to face: "I don't mind feeling it. It's a bit like the smell of damp clothes isn't it?" he asks hopefully.

But later the child's stubborn questioning gets him into a lot of trouble, and he quickly finds out that learning things straight is taken as an act of treachery in the family. He is told the dark secret about a family betrayal involving the IRA but is implicitly forbidden to retell it. He knows, but he will be banished for knowing. Thus after hearing the story from his dying grandfather, the narrator "left him and went straight home, home, where I could never talk to my father or my mother properly again." (Page 126)

But even before this event, very early in his narrative, Deane retells a true story as a lie in order to show how important it is to lie or to deny in order to maintain the family and the community. The protagonist has witnessed the death of a child who was killed by a reversing lorry, the large truck backing up over a little boy. Shortly afterwards a policeman arrives and is so overcome that he vomits.

> I think he felt sick. His distress reached me, airborne, like a smell; in a small vertigo, I sat down on the wall . . . For months, I kept seeing the lorry reversing, and Rory Hannaway's arm going out as he was wound under. Somebody told me that one of the policemen had vomited on the other side of the lorry. I felt the vertigo again on hearing this and, with it, pity for the man. But this seemed wrong; everyone hated the police, told us to stay away from them, that they were a bad lot. So I said nothing, especially as I had felt scarcely anything for Rory's mother or the lorry driver . . ." (Page 11–12).

As it exists, this memory, though true, is unacceptable. It is only when another child retells "in detail how young Rory had been run over by a police car which had not even stopped" (page 12) that the protagonist finds "the subtle sense of treachery I had felt from the start" somehow allayed. The random

152

cruelty of fate is unacceptable, as is a policeman's pain and sympathy for the dead boy and the grieving mother. It is much easier to assign wrong to the police than to fate—or to one's own family, as this child is later asked to do when he learns the truth about his own grandfather and mother.

Although Deane's book is published as a novel, the issues it raises apply also to memoir. The book has been widely assumed to be autobiographical, and even though Deane has said that he knows of three families with the kind of history told in his book, he also admits that large parts of his book are drawn from his own life and that he couldn't have published this book until after the death of his mother.

Reading in the Dark is an important book to examine closely if you too are struggling with shape-shifting stories from the past in your family or community. Deane's book enacts the narrative strategies of concealment and erasure of memory which are in fact its subject, and which are frequent subjects of memoir. For example, the child wrote out the forbidden story in Irish, but in doing so he still revealed nothing:

> I decided to write it all out in an exercise book, partly to get it clear, partly to rehearse it and decide which details to include or leave out. But the fear that someone would find it and read it overcame me. So, with the help of a dictionary, I translated it all into Irish, taking more than a week to do it. Then

I destroyed the English version, burning it in front of my mother's eyes, even though she told me I would clog up the fire with the paper. (Page 194)

The boy reads the Irish essay aloud to his father, who cannot understand it, but "said he liked to hear the language spoken in the house." His mother, who also knows no Irish, nevertheless guesses what her son is doing—revealing that he knows the story, but in a way that the father cannot understand. In the end, we have to believe that the narrator did the only thing he could possibly have done: he kept the mother's secret and participated in the family's silence for many years. But we are also grateful that the story that had to remain unspoken in life could become the powerfully written after death.

"Tell all the truth, but tell it slant," Emily Dickinson cautioned us, echoing Hamlet's famous dictum: "By indirections, find directions out." All the narrative strategies of indirection—multiple tellings, "official" family versions, myths and ghost stories from the past, letters and other documents that contradict memories—are particularly useful in the contemporary memoir. It is precisely the "truth" claims of the form which can make the memoir so rich. The truth is rarely simple and straightforward, families rarely agree on events from the past, and memory itself is slippery. Telling a story in multiple ways enriches it and makes it more interesting, rather than less. And the narrator's voice (yours), musing on the process by which a memory is constructed and reconstructed also adds a new dimension to the telling. I hope you can see, from all this, that many stories can be told, including some family secrets, through these different strategies of indirection.

PERHAPS YOU TOO have a painful story to tell. Maybe it is one which you can only tell to yourself, or write in pencil in a notebook which you keep on a high shelf. Or maybe you will eventually try to publish your story. Only you can decide what it is you want to do. But whatever it is, I hope that this book will help, that it will give you ideas and reassurance and focus—and that it will be a companion to you on your own journey.

EXERCISES

(1) Distinguish between writing for yourself and writing for the eyes of others. Remember you "own" your own truths, and owe nobody an apology if you are writing for yourself alone. Ask family members to respect your privacy and give them the same.

(2) If you want to take your writing one step further and make it available to others, either through publication or private distribution, try to make some other distinctions. List those people who are central

to the narrative and those that are tangential. For those people whose lives are intimately connected with yours or with your story, ask for permission before you share your writing with lots of other people, especially if you wish to publish.

(3) If you are in doubt about whether or not your writing could be construed as libelous, consult an expert in publishing law. There are handbooks which will provide some guidance, for example *The Associated Press Stylebook and Libel Manual*, but remember that this manual is written with reporting in mind where the rules are somewhat different from memoir publishing. If you have a publisher, seek advice from your editor and understand the parts of your contract concerning warranty and indemnification.

Recommended Reading

The following is a list of books which I have found particularly moving or helpful. The list, of course, follows my
own preferences and chance acquaintance and does not
reflect a systematic reading through of the contemporary
memoir. Where the title does not explain the contents, I
have added a brief explanation in parentheses. Included
are the secondary sources mentioned. Books discussed in
the text are preceeded by an asterisk (*).

* Alden, Paulette Bates. *Crossing the Moon: A Journey Through
Infertility*, 1996.
Angelou, Maya. *I Know Why the Caged Bird Sings* (the childhood
of the black writer, dancer, singer, and poet), 1969.
Ascher, Barbara Lazear. *Landscape Without Gravity* (her broth-
er's death from AIDS), 1993.
Baldwin, James. *Notes of a Native Son* (growing up black in
America), 1955.
* Barry, Sebastian. "Note From the Dead," from *Dublines*, Ka-
tie Donovan and Brendan Kennelly, eds., 1996.
Beauvoir, Simone de. *A Very Easy Death* (the death of her
mother), 1985.
Bernstein, Jane. *Loving Rachel* (life with a blind daughter),
1988.

* Boland, Eavan. *Object Lessons: The Life of the Woman and the Poet in Our Time* (memoir of the female Irish poet), 1995.

Busselle, Rebecca. *An Exposure of the Heart* (a photographer's year among the disabled), 1989.

Cary, Lorene. *Black Ice* (a black girl attending an all-white school), 1991.

* Chandler, Marilyn. *A Healing Art; Regeneration Through Autobiography*, 1990.

Clark, Clara Claiborne. *The Seige: the First Eight Years of an Autistic Child's Life* (a mother's account), 1967.

Conroy, Frank. *Stop-Time: The Classic Memoir of Adolescence*, 1965.

* Crews, Harry. *A Childhood: The Biography of a Place*, 1978.

* Deane, Seamus. *Reading in the Dark* (growing up in Derry, Northern Ireland), 1997.

Dew, Robb Forman. *The Family Heart: A Memoir of When Our Son Came Out*, 1994.

Dillard, Annie. *An American Childhood*, 1987.

Dillard, Annie and Cort Conley, eds. *Modern American Memoirs* (an anthology), 1995.

Fields, Wayne. *What the River Knows* (a journey of personal discovery while searching for the origin of a river), 1990.

Finger, Anne. *Past Due: A Story of Disability, Pregnancy, and Birth*, 1990.

Gilbert, Sandra. *Wrongful Death: a Medical Tragedy* (death of her husband), 1995.

Gordon, Mary. *The Shadow Man: A Daughter's Search for Her Father*, 1996.

* Gornick, Vivian. *Fierce Attachments* (mother-daughter ties), 1987.

Graham, Laurie. *Rebuilding the House* (death of her husband), 1990.

* Grealy, Lucy. *Autobiography of a Face* (growing up with cancer and disfigurement), 1994.

Greer, Germaine. *Daddy, We Hardly Knew You* (the search to learn about a dead father), 1989.

Hammer, Signe. *By Her Own Hand: Memoirs of a Suicide's Daughter*, 1991.

Hampl, Patricia. *A Romantic Education* (growing up in St. Paul and journey to Prague), 1981.

Harrison, Kathryn. *The Kiss* (a daughter seduced by her father), 1997.

* Herman, Judith. *Trauma and Recovery*, 1992.

Heron, Echo. *Intensive Care: The Story of a Nurse*, 1987.

Hill, Susan. *Family* (death of a premature child), 1989.

* Hoffman, Eva. *Lost in Translation* (immigration to Canada from Poland), 1989.

Hoffman, Richard. *Half the House* (child abuse), 1995.

Israeloff, Roberta. *In Confidence: Four Years of Therapy*, 1990.

Jamison, Kay Redfield. *An Unquiet Mind: A Memoir of Moods and Madness*, 1995.

Johnson, Fenton. *Geography of the Heart* (death of a gay partner), 1996.

* Kaysen, Susanna. *Girl, Interrupted* (mental illness), 1993.

Karr, Mary. *The Liar's Club* (a troubled childhood with a mentally ill mother), 1995.

Kehoe, Louise. *In This Dark House* (a search to discover the true identity of a father), 1995.

* Kingston, Maxine Hong. *The Woman Warrior: Memoirs of a Girlhood Among Ghosts* (growing up Chinese-American), 1975.

* Kübler-Ross, Elisabeth. *On Death and Dying*, 1969.

Kupfer, Fern. *Before and After Zachariah* (a brain-damaged child), 1982.

* Kusz, Natalie. *Road Song* (growing up in Alaska and survival after a sled-dog attack), 1990.

Landsman, Julie. *Basic Needs: A Year with Street Kids in a City School*, 1993.

Lear, Martha Weinman. *Heart-Sounds: The Story of Love and Loss* (husband's illness and death from heart disease), 1980.

Mairs, Nancy. *Remembering the Bone House* (a personal history told by examining houses lived in, as well as the "bone house," the body), 1989.

* McCarthy, Mary. *Memories of a Catholic Girlhood*, 1957.
* McCourt, Frank. *Angela's Ashes* (a childhood in the slums of Limerick, Ireland), 1996.
* McDonnell, Jane Taylor. *News From the Border: A Mother's Memoir of her Autistic Son*, (with an afterword by Paul McDonnell), 1993.

Millett, Kate. *The Looney-Bin Trip* (struggle with manic-depression and with the authorities), 1990.

Monette, Paul. *Borrowed Time, Becoming a Man*, and *Last Watch of the Night* (a gay man writes of battling AIDS), 1992–1994.

Morrison, Blake. *And When Did You Last See Your Father? A Son's Memoir of Love and Loss*, 1993.

Nyala, Hannah. *Point Last Seen* (a wilderness tracker fleeing an abusive marriage), 1997.

Norris, Kathleen. *Dakota: A Spiritual Geography*, 1993.

Phillips, Jane. *The Magic Daughter: A Memoir of Living with Multiple Personality Disorder*, 1995.

Ratushinskaya, Irina. *Grey Is the Color of Hope* (four years in a Siberian labor camp), 1988.

Rice, Rebecca. *A Time to Mourn: One Woman's Journey Through Widowhood*, 1990.

Rhett, Kathryn. *Survival Stories: Memoirs of Crisis*, 1997.

Rhodes, Richard. *A Hole in the World* (child abuse and neglect), 1990.

Roth, Philip. *Patrimony* (father's death from brain cancer), 1991.

Sacks, Oliver. *A Leg to Stand On* (the famous neurologist writes of his own injury and recovery), 1984.

Schreiber, LeAnne. *Midstream: The Story of a Mother's Death and a Daughter's Renewal*, 1990.

Sidransky, Ruth. *In Silence: Growing up Hearing in a Deaf World*, 1990.

* Steinem, Gloria. "Ruth's Song, Because She Could Not Sing

It," (account of childhood with mentally ill mother), from *Outrageous Acts and Everyday Rebellions*, 1983.

Taylor, Nick. *A Necessary End* (death of parents), 1993.

Walker, Lou Ann. *A Loss for Words: The Story of Deafness in a Family* (growing up as the hearing daughter of deaf parents), 1986.

Wexler, Alice. *Mapping Fate: a Memoir of Family, Risk, and Genetic Research* (a family with Huntingdon's Disease), 1995.

* Wiesel, Elie. *Night* (the survivor of a Nazi death camp), 1960.

Williams, Terry Tempest. *Refuge: An Unnatural History of Family and Place* (cancer deaths and ecology), 1991.

* Wolf, Christa. *A Model Childhood*, (growing up in Nazi Germany), 1980.

Wolff, Geoffrey. *The Duke of Deception: Memories of My Father* (Geoffrey and Tobias are brothers), 1979.

* Wolff, Tobias. *This Boy's Life* (child abuse and escape), 1989.

FOR THE BEST IN PAPERBACKS, LOOK FOR THE 🐧

In every corner of the world, on every subject under the sun, Penguin represents quality and variety—the very best in publishing today.

For complete information about books available from Penguin—including Puffins, Penguin Classics, and Arkana—and how to order them, write to us at the appropriate address below. Please note that for copyright reasons the selection of books varies from country to country.

In the United Kingdom: Please write to *Dept. JC, Penguin Books Ltd, FREEPOST, West Drayton, Middlesex UB7 0BR.*

If you have any difficulty in obtaining a title, please send your order with the correct money, plus ten percent for postage and packaging, to *P.O. Box No. 11, West Drayton, Middlesex UB7 0BR*

In the United States: Please write to *Consumer Sales, Penguin USA, P.O. Box 999, Dept. 17109, Bergenfield, New Jersey 07621-0120.* VISA and MasterCard holders call 1-800-253-6476 to order all Penguin titles

In Canada: Please write to *Penguin Books Canada Ltd, 10 Alcorn Avenue, Suite 300, Toronto, Ontario M4V 3B2*

In Australia: Please write to *Penguin Books Australia Ltd, P.O. Box 257, Ringwood, Victoria 3134*

In New Zealand: Please write to *Penguin Books (NZ) Ltd, Private Bag 102902, North Shore Mail Centre, Auckland 10*

In India: Please write to *Penguin Books India Pvt Ltd, 706 Eros Apartments, 56 Nehru Place, New Delhi 110 019*

In the Netherlands: Please write to *Penguin Books Netherlands bv, Postbus 3507, NL-1001 AH Amsterdam*

In Germany: Please write to *Penguin Books Deutschland GmbH, Metzlerstrasse 26, 60594 Frankfurt am Main*

In Spain: Please write to *Penguin Books S.A., Bravo Murillo 19, 1° B, 28015 Madrid*

In Italy: Please write to *Penguin Italia s.r.l., Via Felice Casati 20, I-20124 Milano*

In France: Please write to *Penguin France S.A., 17 rue Lejeune, F-31000 Toulouse*

In Japan: Please write to *Penguin Books Japan, Ishikiribashi Building, 2-5-4, Suido, Bunkyo-ku, Tokyo 112*

In Greece: Please write to *Penguin Hellas Ltd, Dimocritou 3, GR-106 71 Athens*

In South Africa: Please write to *Longman Penguin Southern Africa (Pty) Ltd, Private Bag X08, Bertsham 2013*